PAINTING CHINA & PORCELAIN

PAINTING
CHINA & PORCELAIN

SHEILA SOUTHWELL

David & Charles

DEDICATION

This one is for you, Mom and Dad.

ACKNOWLEDGEMENTS

Thank you to Harry Fraser

A DAVID & CHARLES BOOK

Text copyright © Sheila Southwell 1995
Photography and layouts
copyright © David & Charles Publishers 1995

Book design Diana Knapp

First published 1995

A catalogue record for this book is available from the British Library.

ISBN 0 7153 0283 3

Typeset by Greenshires Icon
and printed in Italy by LEGO SpA
for David & Charles
Brunel House   Newton Abbot   Devon

CONTENTS

PREFACE

*Happy are the painters for they shall not be lonely. Light and colour
and peace and hope will keep them company to the end, or almost
to the end, of the day. I know of nothing which more entirely
absorbs the mind.*

WINSTON CHURCHILL

Twenty-six years ago, when my children started school and I had a little time to myself, I decided I would start studying a painting technique. Having had no art training, I was at a loss as to what I should study. I liked the idea of watercolours but, whilst still undecided, I met a student of china painting who informed me that it was the most interesting of the fine arts and that I should at least try it.

I was not convinced that this was for me but went along to a class to see how I liked it. I am glad that I did because that first lesson was to change my whole life. What started as a hobby developed into a full-time profession as I became involved in teaching, lecturing and writing – this is my fourth book on the subject. China painting has taken up all of my spare time for the last twenty-six years – the desire to try watercolours has had to wait.

My first book ran to five editions before going out of print. Due to a continuing demand from all over the world, it was decided to publish a much up-dated version with lots of new projects, in full colour, and this book is the result. During the last fifteen years, more materials have become available – these are included in this new and exciting book. There is also a section on the non-fire acrylic colours for those who would like to paint on china but do not have access to a kiln.

China painting is a fascinating medium in which to work – every time that I open the kiln I experience a fresh sense of excitement. Over the years I have met interesting people from all over the world and have made many good friends. To see my students progressing and going on to teach and share their knowledge is very rewarding. My husband, Alan, is very interested in the world of china painting and has typed the manuscript of this book, for which I am very grateful. Was there ever a time before china painting?

INTRODUCTION

Porcelain was first made in the eighth century by the Chinese who kept the method of its manufacture a closely guarded secret. European potters, seeing pieces brought back from the Orient, tried unsuccessfully for several centuries to copy this beautiful ware with its translucent quality. It was to be the Meissen factory in Germany which first manufactured porcelain in 1709 and, despite attempts to keep the secret, it was not long before potters all over Europe were producing it. Some of the best early examples come from France, England and Italy, as well as Germany.

Bone china was to come a little later, in the eighteenth century. It is a softer type of porcelain to which is added calcified animal bone, hence the name. At this time everything was handpainted but with the introduction of transfers in the late eighteenth century, gradually less was done by hand. Today only a tiny proportion of factory pieces are decorated by hand; almost all the china sold in the shops is decorated with transfers, even the limited edition pieces. The reason for this should become obvious when I describe the painting process, which can be quite lengthy for special pieces. One exception to the rule is figurines, which tend to be decorated by hand, at least in part.

China paint is quite different from all other mediums although it does share some properties with oils and watercolours as the powdered colours are mixed with an oil-based medium, and they appear transparent (like watercolour) on application. Here, however, the similarity ends.

The pigments used for china painting are manufactured from mineral oxides and precious metals and are called onglaze (or overglaze) enamels. These are made to fuse with the glaze on the china by firing at a temperature of approximately 1436°F (780°C). The glaze melts and absorbs the colours which, after cooling, are firmly sealed.

Usually, the pieces have to be painted and fired several times to build up a depth of colour. If colours are applied too thickly they can blister during the firing process and impair the beautiful translucency familiar to bone china. They are therefore applied in washes, working from the lightest to the darkest, rather like watercolour painting. If the painter tries to complete the piece by painting and firing once, the result will be a design which looks flat and uninteresting (except in the case of special techniques which require only one fire). For very special portraits, landscapes and complex designs, the pieces often need to be painted and fired several times.

China Painting Basics

In this first part of the book I cover all the basic background information you need to know in order to paint china successfully. Here I explain the materials you will need, how to apply the colour to the china, and how to fire your finished piece. For those of you just starting out, I also take a look at non-fire paints, and the basic rules of colour and design. Once you have worked your way through this section you will be more than ready to tackle the specially designed projects given later in the book.

MATERIALS AND EQUIPMENT

Y ou do not need to buy all of the materials and tools mentioned in this chapter – only the essential items (see below) are needed initially, and you can then start painting right away.

CHINA AND PORCELAIN

Throughout this book I will be referring to china and porcelain. These two terms can be confusing, so deserve further explanation.

China is a general term used by the layman; in fact the ware used by china painters is known as bone china. Most bone china is made in England and is composed of china clay, bone and feldspar. Porcelain, on the other hand, is made in Europe and Japan – indeed the Japanese are renowned for their pretty porcelain shapes. Porcelain is composed of kaolin, quartz and feldspar. Bone china and porcelain vary slightly in appearance. Bone china has a much whiter appearance, while porcelain is usually off-white. Porcelain also has a slightly more matt surface.

Both materials are suitable for painting on but they must be brand new. What we refer to as china blanks may be used – these are pieces of fired and glazed ware which are made especially to be decorated at a later stage, professionally or by hobbyists. China purchased from second-hand shops would not be suitable. Earthenware is unsuitable as it can develop black damp spots and blister with tiny bubbles in the glaze during firing.

China and porcelain are decorated in the same way. Pigment mixed with oil is painted on to the glazed piece. When it is fired to the correct temperature, the pigment fuses with the glaze and the oil burns off. The glossy high glaze on bone china is softer than that on porcelain, enabling it to accept colour more readily.

FIRING TEMPERATURES

Bone china and porcelain should be fired at slightly different temperatures. Ideally, porcelain should be fired between 1472–1562°F (800–850°C) and bone china between 1418–1436°F (770–780°C). If the kiln is not hot enough the colours will not mature, and will look dull and lifeless. However, I often fire both together at 1436°F (780°C), putting the porcelain at the top of the kiln, which is the hottest part, and the bone china at the bottom. Because of their softer glaze, bone china objects will stick together on firing if allowed to touch. Porcelain will not stick together and you can, for instance, fire porcelain boxes with the lids in place. However, if in doubt play safe and fire the lids separately.

ONGLAZE ENAMELS

Onglaze enamel is the name given to china paint. It is sold in powdered form, and is

---

MATERIALS FOR ONGLAZE ENAMELS

ESSENTIAL ITEMS
bone china or porcelain
onglaze colours
pure turpentine
mediums for mixing and
   painting
two white tiles
flexible palette knife
sable or squirrel hair brushes
tracing paper
Stabilo china pencil
waterproof felt tip pen
pen oil and mapping pen
methylated spirits

kitchen towels
cotton or nylon overall
access to a kiln

OPTIONAL ITEMS
masking materials
self-adhesive film
graphite paper
wipe-out tool
covered palette
synthetic foam pad
square of pure silk
cotton wool

mixed with a medium (see below). There are hundreds of beautiful colours from which to choose, so make sure that you buy the best – they only cost a little more. Also, always ensure that you use the colours with no gritty particles, those which have been ground very smoothly during their manufacture.

The colours are made from mineral oxides and precious metals, and fuse with the glaze when fired at the correct temperature. Some onglaze colours contain lead, but it is hoped that completely lead-free colours will be available in the near future. Most colours change very little during the firing process. The pink and purple colours contain more gold and therefore they are known as the 'gold

colours'. These are more expensive than the other colours and, if possible, require a slightly hotter fire to mature properly.

Most colours can be mixed together except for cadmium colours (see below).

REDS

Reds cause more trouble than any other colour and therefore require further explanation. There are two types of red – iron red and cadmium red. The iron reds present no problem and can be mixed and fired as other colours. However, the cadmium colours, usually the very bright reds and oranges, need to be handled more carefully. They contain cadmium and selenium and, if there is the tiniest trace of another colour on the china or the brush,

A selection of materials needed for painting china and porcelain with onglaze enamels.

the red will be bleached off during the firing. Once this happens it is almost impossible to rectify as the surface will be distorted with a dirty appearance. These colours need a lower firing, at approximately 1400°F (760°C). The cadmium reds are usually more difficult to apply – they are best used for solid blocks of colour and should be applied more heavily than usual. Some of the yellows contain cadmium and therefore behave in the same way. The cadmium colours are inter-mixable with each other and are best reserved for occasional use. The iron reds are less bright but, as they can be mixed with other colours (yellow, for example), are more reliable than the cadmium colours.

The cadmium colours can usually be identified by their names – for example Santa Claus red, pillar box red, and scarlet, all of which suggest bright colours. The iron reds have names such as yellow red, Derby red, Meissen red, and Pompadour.

A CAUTIONARY NOTE

Onglaze colours are toxic and should not be put in the mouth in any way; they are most dangerous in the powdered form. Any spilled colour should be wiped up immediately with a wet cloth or tissue, and a face mask should be worn if you are using a large quantity of powdered colour, for instance when groundlaying (see page 58). The small amounts of colour mixed with the medium should present no problem when treated sensibly.

WATER-BASED COLOURS

These are tubes of ceramic onglaze colours which have to be fired in a kiln at the normal temperature of 770–850°C. They are fine for beginners but most experienced china painters dislike their lack of shading ability – ie they lack the tonal flexibility of the oil-based colours.

NON-FIRE COLOURS

These are mostly acrylic colours which are water based. They do not need to be fired in a kiln. They are not permanent so they should *not* be painted on to items used for food or drink. These colours are for decorative use only, and are not suitable for ceramics in general use. They are discussed in more detail on page 13.

TURPENTINE

In china painting turpentine has two functions. It is used as a cleaning agent for brushes and china, and occasionally it is used for thinning colours. Only pure spirits of turpentine should be used – not the house-hold variety. If you are allergic to turpentine there is a fragrant-smelling alternative available called limidex. Turpentine is the main ingredient of fat oil.

MEDIUMS (OILS) FOR MIXING AND PAINTING

Mediums are used for two purposes – mixing the colours and applying them to the surface. The powdered colours are mixed with a medium to reach a 'toothpaste' consistency, but the brush needs to be lubricated with a clean oil in order for the mixed colours to flow easily onto the china. Whichever oil you use will burn off during the firing, leaving only the onglaze colour on the china.

OIL-BASED MEDIUMS

Probably the most commonly used mediums, these are either vegetable- or mineral- (petroleum) based and all possess different qualities. For example, some dry very quickly (closed mediums) while others will not dry until fired (open mediums). These individual qualities can be put to special use. Oils distilled from plants such as cloves, lavender and aniseed, known as ethereal oils, can be added to the thicker, fast-drying oils to retard the drying process and to make a thinner consistency for painting. Because these oils burn away completely during the firing process the one you choose is really a personal preference. The solvent used for all these oil-based mediums is turpentine.

Closed mediums (fast-drying)

Fat oil Fat oil is the most common fast-drying medium and is a strong, oily resin made by evaporating pure turpentine. It dries extremely quickly but this can be slowed down by adding one of the ethereal oils such as cloves or lavender. It is excellent when used to apply strong colours for one-fire decorating techniques (see page 00). Fat oil has been used in the china painting industry for two centuries and is still their most-used oil. It can be toxic and occasionally people develop allergies to the turpentine – fortunately, there are some excellent alternatives such as water-based mediums (see below).

Balsam of copaiba This viscous vegetable-based oil is extremely popular with china painters. It is fairly fast-drying but can be mixed with other vegetables or ethereal oils such as olive or lavender, to keep it open (workable).

Oscar oil A superior quality but expensive thick oil.

Open mediums (non-drying)

Open mediums do not dry until fired; therefore colours mixed with them stay open (or workable) indefinitely. Most of my work is done using open mediums. They can be used both for mixing the powdered paint and as the medium for applying colours. Some painters also use them instead of turpentine to clean their brushes. These oils can be left safely on the brushes, which helps to keep them supple.

Olive oil An excellent medium for mixing colours – you can mix large quantities of powdered colour with this oil and store it in dust-proof containers where it will keep fresh indefinitely. However, another oil should be used as the painting medium. If olive oil is used for both mixing and painting, it will be too wet. An oil with a little more 'body', such as copaiba, should be used to apply the colour.

Glycerine An odourless, non-toxic oil which is non-drying and available cheaply from your pharmacist. It is water-based.

Liquid paraffin A non-drying mineral-based oil.

Baby oil A non-toxic, non-drying oil which contains liquid paraffin.

Sewing machine oil A mineral-based oil popular with some painters. It can be mixed with other mineral oils.

Lavender oil A fragrant, ethereal oil which is expensive. The cheaper spike lavender is fine to use – it is 'spiked' with camphor oil.

Aniseed oil An ethereal oil which makes an excellent medium for penwork.

Clove oil An ethereal oil with a very cloying smell. It is excellent for thinning other oils.

WATER-BASED MEDIUMS

There is an excellent range of water-based mediums now available. They are recommended for people who are allergic to oil- and turpentine-based mediums. First developed by the Royal Copenhagen Porcelain factory in Denmark, they are referred to as RCP mediums. They are used in exactly the same way as other mediums but the thinning solvent is water instead of turpentine.

COMMERCIALLY PREPARED MEDIUMS

These are prepared by professional teachers and commercial companies. They are excellent and ready for use. There is a large number available from suppliers and it is really a matter of choice which one you prefer.

MAKING YOUR OWN MEDIUM

Of course you can experiment by mixing various oils together until you find a suitable painting mix that you like. Try mixing together 8 parts balsam of copaiba, 1 part oil of lavender and 1 part oil of cloves and then shake together. If the resulting liquid is too thin, add more copaiba – if it is too thick, add more lavender. Mix the powdered colour with olive oil or a similar non-drying medium. Have fun!

OTHER ESSENTIAL ITEMS

White tiles These are ideal to use as a palette for mixing and storing the colours.

MATERIALS LIST

water
graphite pencil
kitchen towels
tile for colour mixing
non-fire colours
ceramic objects on which
    to paint
various brushes

TIPS

1 Water is the solvent for most non-fire colours.
2 Allow sufficient baking time to set the colours properly.
3 Never allow the painted areas to come into contact with food or drink.
4 A layer of varnish gives extra protection to the colour.
5 Do not use on tiled surfaces which are cleaned regularly with abrasive cleaners.
6 Do not fire these colours in a kiln – they are designed for baking in an ordinary oven.
7 The colours are very versatile, easy to use, fully inter-mixable.
8 Wash brushes thoroughly in water after use.
9 Replace lids properly on the paints after use.
10 Remember – these colours do not sink under the glaze. They sit on top and are therefore not permanent.

Many people would love to decorate china but have absolutely no access to a kiln. Non-fire colours are freely available from craft shops, and are a very good and inexpensive way of getting started. Although they cannot be filtered or used for shading they are fun to use, and some lovely objects can be designed. Many of the projects in this book can be tried out using non-fire paints, and although your results will look very different to the fired paints, you will, I am sure, be pleased with the finished item.

APPLYING NON-FIRE PAINTS

The non-fire colours are acrylic, water-based and are extremely easy to apply. They are not permanent and should not be used to decorate pieces which are to come into contact with food, drink or your mouth.

Non-fire ceramic paints and their varnishes must be used in well-ventilated areas. They are available in many different colours which mix well together and can be painted on to any ceramic surface, including pottery and earthenware, and in fact can also be used on glass. They can be applied with a brush (nylon ones are best), a sponge, or with materials such as clingfilm or tissue paper, to create intriguing and original effects. They also pass through an airbrush very well.

The colours have to be allowed to dry, preferably overnight, and should then be placed in a domestic oven for $^3/_4$ to 2 hours at a temperature of 356–392°F (180–200°C). Always refer to the manufacturer's instructions for precise instructions regarding this stage.

One colour can be painted over another, baking between each layer. Masking materials such as Fablon can be used to create stencils or you can buy special stencil paper and use this to create patterns of your choice. If you want to make a straight line, apply some sticky tape, paint the colour over it then remove the tape. Once the colours are dry, apply a clear varnish for extra protection.

Non-fire colours can be useful for 'touching up' small areas of regular onglaze decorated pieces if you do not wish or need to fire them again. They are also useful for covering small chips in the paint. You will find all sorts of uses for these acrylics, as they produce areas of bright, opaque colour.

Have fun with non-fire paints but do not regard them as absolutely permanent; they are for decoration only. Hopefully they will inspire you to progress to the fine art of china painting in the traditional way.

Flexible palette knife This is used for mixing the powdered colours with the oils. It should be quite narrow; this will make it easier to handle. After use, clean the knife with turpentine to avoid rusting.

Brushes See pages 20–1.

Tracing paper For transferring designs.

Stabilo china pencil Also known as a chinagraph, this soft graphite pencil is used to sketch designs on to china, and will burn away during firing.

Waterproof felt tip pen These are ideal for drawing on china but it is essential that you buy one with a very fine point. Will fire away.

Pen oil and mapping pen These are needed for the technique of penwork (see page 42–3). The best pen oil is one which is aniseed based for mixing with colour to give a good, consistent flow through a fine pen. The oil is mixed with the chosen pigment before being used with the pen. Pens should have a fine, firm nib with a fine point.

There are many commercially prepared pen mediums available. Some will dry before firing, and some will not. Some are oil based, some water based. ES Outlining Oil No. 178 is an aniseed based oil which mixes with powdered onglaze colours to an indian ink consistency. It will dry in 20 to 30 minutes; thin if necessary with a little turpentine. Liquid artificial sweetener, mixed with powdered colour, will flow smoothly from the pen. It does not dry until fired, and will thin down with water. Icing sugar can also be used as a medium. Mix powdered onglaze colour with $1/3$ icing sugar and dilute with water for a very fast-drying pen medium. Icing sugar tends to clog the pen, so clean the nib regularly with water. Cola, or other sugary drinks, can be mixed with powdered colour to make a fast-drying pen medium. Again, clean the pen nib regularly to prevent clogging.

Methylated spirit This is used for cleaning china before painting, as it evaporates quickly. However, if your china happens to be exceptionally dirty it is better to use soap and water. Methylated spirit is also useful for cleaning brushes after using lustres and gold.

Kitchen towels These should be lint-free. They are used for cleaning brushes and other materials.

Cotton or nylon overall This is needed to prevent fibres from your clothing from coming into contact with the wet paint. It is an absolute essential.

Access to a kiln Access to a kiln is essential (unless you are using non-fire paints), because without the correct heat application the colours you have painted will not be permanent. The use of kilns is covered on pages 26–9. If you do not have a kiln of your own, your teacher, if you have one, will fire your china for you. If you do not have a teacher, then try your local adult education college. They usually have a pottery class with a kiln, which the pottery teacher may be willing to fire for you. Alternatively, any of the china painting materials suppliers listed on page 124–5 will be pleased to fire your pieces. As a last resort, look in your telephone directory to find your nearest friendly potter.

OPTIONAL ITEMS

Masking materials These are used to mask (or cover) the areas which you do not wish to paint, usually to reserve a white area for later decoration. There are two types of material available; the one most commonly used is a thick liquid which is usually deep pink, deep blue or green in colour. Use an old brush to apply it to the area to be masked out, paint it on quite thickly and allow to dry completely – about 20 to 30 minutes. This will dry to a plastic film which can then be painted over quite safely. It is important to remove the film before firing. To remove, lift the corner with an old pen nib and it should peel away in one piece – lovely!

The other type of masking material comes in a powdered form which has to be mixed with water until quite thick. Paint on to the surface to be masked and allow to dry. This masking material has the advantage of being able to withstand the heat of the kiln so it can be fired several times without harm. Remove by washing off or rubbing

with a soft cloth after firing. This type of masking is ideal to use for complicated designs where the peel-off one would be difficult to remove from intricate patterns.

Self-adhesive films These can be used to create stencils – Contact, Fablon or similar materials are the most popular. Simply attach to the surface you wish to be masked out. After use, the shapes can be stuck back on to their backing film and used again.

Graphite paper This is used for tracing designs on to china. It is similar to carbon paper but has a graphite covering and is far superior. Nowadays there are some excellent graphite papers available from china painting suppliers – if you buy them anywhere else check you are not being given carbon paper.

Wipe-out tool A tool with a rubber point at both ends, used for taking out sharp lines or highlights. A sharpened rubber pencil works well, too.

Covered palette There are several ready-made palettes on the market. But a shallow tin with a lid and a piece of glass cut to fit the bottom is just as good – the most important thing is to keep the mixed paint free from dust and lint. If you do a lot of painting, it is worth mixing large quantities of colour to be kept in a separate palette and then just take out the colours on a tile as you need them. This way, you will keep your 'stockpile' of colour free from extra oil and dust contamination.

Synthetic foam pad These are available with a beautifully fine texture and are used for blending painted colours very smoothly, especially in portraits. Cosmetic sponges are a cheap alternative, available from your pharmacist. To clean, just soak in turpentine (I keep a special jar for this), wash in a good detergent, then rinse and dry thoroughly.

Square of pure silk Use a 6 inch (15cm) square wrapped around a wad of cotton wool to pad painted-on colour in order to obtain a smooth background. The fabric must be very finely woven so that no grain marks are left on the china. After use, wash it with warm soapy water and iron out all the creases.

Cotton wool Used to make the silk pad.

READY TO START

Once you have collected all your materials together you will be ready to start. Put on your cotton or nylon overall, then clean the china thoroughly before you commence work and before you start to mix paints. Use methylated spirit to do this – if the china is particularly dirty you may need to use soap and water. Dust is your biggest enemy. One of my first mistakes was to attend a class wearing an angora sweater; I was hastily covered in an old shirt before I could start to shed fibres over everyone's work!

Whilst you are not using your mixed paints it is essential to keep out dust, so place them in a covered box or put an upturned plate over them. If dust is allowed to collect on the wet painted china the paint will collect around the particles and leave little spots of piled colour, spoiling the finished piece. The dust will burn away in the kiln but small residues of colour will remain.

It is good practice to place a piece of old, thick towelling over your knees while painting. This will protect your clothing and is useful to remove excess turpentine from the brush. Always keep your working area clean and uncluttered and place a sheet of polythene on the work table. I cannot stress enough how important cleanliness is in china painting if muddy and distorted colours are to be avoided.

Have about $^1/_2$–$^3/_4$in (1–2cm) of turpentine ready in a jar to clean brushes and change it when it gets dirty. You can re-use turpentine by leaving it covered overnight; dirty sediment will settle on the bottom of the jar and the clean turpentine can then be poured off and re-used. This way, a bottle of turpentine will last a long time. Work in a good light – on dull days use a daylight bulb. Always lay out the work space in the same way, with your turpentine close to hand and not at the back of the table so you have to reach across.

MIXING THE COLOURS

Using a small, flexible palette knife grind a little of your powdered colour with sufficient medium to a smooth 'toothpaste' consistency on a clean white tile. If the mixture falls off the palette knife when you shake it upside down it is not thick enough, so add a little more colour. If mixed correctly, the paint should stay on the palette knife when shaken firmly. Transfer the mixed colours to a palette or separate tile – never mix and store colours on the same tile as you will only succeed in transferring powdered pigment from one colour to another. Place the colours in the same sequence on the palette each time; this way you know where each colour is. Include several different hues of each colour, starting from the lightest through to the darkest.

Unlike their predecessors, modern powdered colours are finely ground and easy to mix.

TRANSFERRING THE DESIGN

Before starting to paint, you will need a clear outline on your china from which to work. There are several ways of achieving this. You can, of course, sketch the design straight on to the surface of the china with a Stabilo chinagraph pencil, but unless you are an excellent draughtsman it is easier to use one of the alternative methods of tracing. If you keep sketching and erasing, your china will become greasy and will not be a good surface on which to paint.

I have placed these alternative methods in order of my own preference, in terms of accuracy and speed. Whichever method you use, it is better to draw the design on to cartridge paper first and make sure that you are completely happy with it. Then trace it with good quality tracing paper and use this to apply the design on to the china.

GRAPHITE PAPER METHOD

Graphite paper comes in several colours and has the advantage of leaving a clean, sharp line which can be painted over with care. Pale grey graphite paper is excellent. The paper can be re-used.

GRAPHITE PAPER METHOD

❈ Clean the china and lay the graphite paper (graphite-side down) on the china.
❈ Place the sketch that you wish to transfer over the graphite paper and secure with sticky tape.
❈ Using a sharp ball point pen or stylus, press through the design on to the china – make sure that you have covered all the design lines. If you use a red pen you can easily see if you have missed any.
❈ Remove the graphite paper and you will now have a perfectly transferred design (unless you placed the graphite paper the wrong way up, which can be infuriating!).

STABILO CHINAGRAPH PENCIL METHOD

STABILO CHINAGRAPH PENCIL METHOD

❧ Trace your chosen design with tracing paper cut to an appropriate size, then scribble over the reverse of the traced drawing with a Stabilo chinagraph pencil.

❧ Place the tracing, scribbled side down, on to the china and fix securely with sticky tape. Re-trace the pattern with a sharp stylus or ball point pen.

❧ Remove any excess graphite from the china with a soft brush.

FELT TIP PEN METHOD

This type of pen is excellent for applying designs when the wipe-out method is to be used (page 40), as the wet background can be safely painted over it. The main drawback to using a felt tip pen is that all too often the lines are so well defined that the painter neglects to establish all the proper highlights and shading. This can mean that after firing there is a group of flowers or leaves in the design which have not been properly defined. Before firing you must imagine what the design is going to look like when these outlines have been fired away.

❧ Using tracing paper trace your design on to the china.

❧ Draw over all the lines with a very fine waterproof felt tip pen. This will dry very quickly and can then be painted over without smudging. All the lines from the felt tip will disappear on firing.

❧ If the marks remain after firing, you are not firing to a hot enough temperature.

POWDERING-ON METHOD

Use this technique if you need a light fired-on outline to work from. It does require a little practice to perfect. Wear a face mask for this method.

❧ Use the graphite paper method to position the design on the china.

❧ With finely ground grey onglaze colour, brush a little loose powder over the graphite marks – the powder will stick only to the waxy graphite design.

❧ Remove all the excess powder with a soft brush, taking all the usual care, and fire at 1436°F (780°C). The fine outline which remains will be permanent. (This method is very useful for demonstrators who may need to use the same plate several times at demonstrations.)

POWDERING-ON METHOD

FELT TIP PEN METHOD

BRUSHES AND BRUSH STROKES

The basic brush strokes demonstrated on pages 22–4 should be mastered as early as possible. The correct use of these brush strokes, together with good colour mixing, is the basis for all successful china paintings and will teach you to use two confident strokes instead of ten hesitant ones. Practise them with gouache or poster colour on dark paper, using different sized brushes before trying them on china.

Only the best brushes will do if you are to achieve success in china painting. The brushes used are either sable or squirrel hair (which is a cheaper alternative to sable). Synthetic brushes are too stiff for general china painting but are useful for applying lustres as they have the advantage of not shedding loose hairs.

Brushes must be well-shaped with no stray hairs protruding, and should be soft and pliable. Brushes you already possess which have been used for other types of painting (oils, acrylics, and so on) are not suitable. Pointed brushes should have a good point.

When buying a brush, dispose of the clear plastic tip protector if it has one as it can damage the brush badly if not replaced carefully. Brushes with these protectors on should be closely inspected in the art shop before buying, as they often create stray hairs where customers have replaced them carelessly.

Flat brushes should have a chisel-straight edge with even lengths of hair showing. When using, if the brush separates at the end and 'opens like a mouth', you probably have a faulty brush. If after conditioning and shaping with soft oil, such as olive oil, it refuses to stay flat in use, you may be able to get it exchanged as sometimes there are too many hairs in the brush and they get twisted in the ferrule during manufacture. Before using a brand new brush, first wash in pure turpentine and dry with a soft cloth.

TYPES OF BRUSHES

FLAT SHADER   Used completely flattened for applying backgrounds and for painting designs. Surprisingly delicate and detailed work can be accomplished with these brushes. Sizes range from 1/4in to 1 1/2in (6mm to 38mm).

MOP BRUSH   A large, soft brush, excellent for blending large areas.

RIGGER   A brush with long, tapering hairs, originally used to paint ships' rigging – hence its name!

CONDITIONING YOUR BRUSH

If you treat your brushes with care, they will give you years of service. Before each use, condition the brush by wiggling and shaping in a medium such as olive oil, placed on a clean, flat tile. The oil should reach up to the brush ferrule. Next, gently squeeze out all excess oil on to soft tissue or cloth and re-shape the brush with your fingers. It is now ready for use.

CLEANING YOUR BRUSH

Something I learned during my very first lesson in china painting was that no matter how late in the day it is, or how tired you are, it is imperative to clean and condition the brush thoroughly after use. To clean your brush, wash it gently in turpentine, wipe dry, then condition and shape as described above. Place the brush in a dust-free container, and it will stay soft and pliable indefinitely. For those who are allergic to turpentine, an alternative called limidex (which smells deliciously of oranges) is available. If you use a soft, open medium to paint with (see page 14) you may also use it to clean and condition your brushes, and need never use turpentine.

There is no excuse for hard, paint-encrusted brushes – they suggest lazy, sloppy habits. If, however, you do have an old brush which is hardened with dried paint, it can usually be revived with a wash in turpentine, but bear in mind that once brushes become hard they start to shed hairs, and they may already be not worth restoring.

STORING BRUSHES

Brushes should always be stored in a dustproof container when not in use, making sure that the hairs will not be damaged. They can be pushed through bamboo or woven table mats and carefully rolled up. I keep mine upright in jars and cover the jars with rigid cardboard cylinders about 4in (10cm) taller than the largest brush. This allows good air circulation but keeps out the moths and dust. One dry, hot summer I left my brushes uncovered for several weeks and it took me a long time to remove all the dust from them.

POINTER   Used for general painting, several sizes of pointer are needed. Sizes range from 000 to 10.

LONG POINTER   A brush with extra-long hairs, useful for scrolling and detailed work. Available in various sizes.

CAT'S TONGUE   A short, flat brush with a rounded, tongue-shaped end.

CUT LINER   A brush with long, diagonally cut hair which is used mainly for painting lines around plates on a banding wheel.

STIPPLER   A stippler has a short, blunt edge used for textured filling-in of colour, painting foliage in scenes, and portraiture. Available in several sizes.

BLENDING BRUSH   A most important brush, which is used for smoothing and blending paint strokes. Any soft, full brush can be reserved for blending; I have them in several sizes and keep them especially for this purpose.

TINTING BRUSH   Usually short-haired and flat. Used for backgrounds, sizes range from ¼in to 1½in (6mm to 38mm).

FULL LOADING
This is used when the brush stroke is to be of an even colour throughout. The brush is first dipped into the painting medium and then pushed into the pile of colour, taking up an even amount at the end of the brush. The resulting stroke will be of uniform tone.

SIDE LOADING
This is usually done with a flat shader (see page 20). Only one side of the brush is loaded with paint. First dip the tip of the brush into the painting medium and then push the flat brush into the colour so that only one side of the brush takes up the paint. The resulting stroke will have a graduated tone, with more colour on one side than the other. This is very useful for adding darker shadows under turned back leaves and petals.

DOUBLE LOADING
This is also done with a flat shader. The brush is in fact shaded with two colours. This is achieved by side loading with a colour on one side as outlined above, then side loading a different colour on the other side. The resulting stroke will be two-toned and is useful for painting leaves.

LOADING THE BRUSH

The type of stroke you wish to paint can determine the way in which you load the brush. The three most common ways are full, side and double loading.

BRUSH STROKES

Your brush is your best friend, and the strokes you make with it will determine your proficiency as a china painter. Good brush strokes are the foundation of painting; trying to paint without learning how they are formed is like trying to build a house without foundations.

The thickness of the brush stroke will depend both on the size brush you use and the amount of pressure applied when painting. Naturally, a light pressure will produce a thinner stroke than a heavier pressure. Practise different brush strokes with light, medium and heavy pressure and see how they vary.

It is always better to hold the china in your hand, turning it as you go so that the brush strokes are always painted towards you. Turn the china upside-down and from side to side and let the brush do the work for you. Do not be afraid to use the whole brush, not just the tip. Practise pressing and lifting the brush so that you achieve a good, tapered stroke.

The most frequently used strokes
- the comma stroke
- the 'c' stroke
- the flat stroke

They are all demonstrated opposite. Practise them whenever you can – the more you practise the better you will be. Aim to achieve clean, even strokes in one movement. If you run out of colour before the end of a stroke add a little more oil to the brush. Always take a fresh load of paint for each stroke. Remember, each time you make a stroke with your brush it is part of the learning process – each stroke takes you nearer to perfection! Get into the habit of practising a few strokes before every painting session – and enjoy them.

COMMA STROKE

This stroke is useful for painting backgrounds around the main design (using a flat brush) and for shaping leaves and flowers.

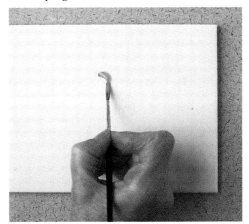 

1 Hold the brush reasonably upright. Balance your hand on the surface to be painted, and begin the stroke by gently pressing the brush hairs down to form a rounded shape.
2 Begin to pull the stroke in a gentle curve, releasing pressure as you pull. Slow down as you make the thinner tail of the stroke, and stop briefly before lifting the brush off. This gives a nice clean finish to the stroke.

'C' STROKE

Possibly the most used stroke in china painting. It is used for all types of china painting, especially for 'framing up' around a design. This stroke always begins and ends on the tip of the brush.

1 Begin by holding the brush upright and make contact with the surface. Slowly begin to pull the brush round in a curve, whilst applying more pressure.
2 As you pass the mid-point of the curve, begin releasing pressure, and continue to do so to the end of the stroke. Halt briefly and lift off the brush.

STRAIGHT STROKE

The straight stroke is painted with a large, square brush and is used for laying in backgrounds. Short, regular strokes give a better effect.

1 To paint straight strokes successfully, press down cleanly with the brush, but not so hard as to fan the bristles.
2 Draw the brush towards you, and lift up quickly. Repeat as often as is necessary to cover the area.

FILTERING STROKE

'Filtering' is a method of blending individual strokes. Flat strokes are applied randomly (left) and the same brush is then used very lightly to blend them together (right). If the brush is held towards the end of its shaft, a lighter stroke is achieved. This will just 'fan' the paint, giving a slightly textured background. Different colours may be filtered together. Avoid having any hard edges of colour.

BLENDING STROKES

This technique will eliminate individual brush marks altogether, and give a soft, even layer of colour with no harsh edges. A very soft, fluffy brush (a mop brush is ideal) must be used for this technique. Colour should be applied as evenly as possible, using a flat brush (left). The blending brush is then gently stroked over the wet paint, eliminating any uneven brush marks (right). As soon as it picks up too much colour (it will start to create its own stroke marks at this point) it should be cleaned with a fast-drying solvent such as methylated spirits and fluffed up again on a soft cloth.

APPLYING COLOUR TO THE DESIGN

Lay out your palette in the same order each time, with colours going from light to dark. By doing this, you will automatically know where each colour is when you want it.

If using an 'open' medium (one which does not dry until fired) you can use this one medium both to mix and to apply the colours. If you are mixing with a fast-drying medium (such as fat oil or copaiba) you will need a softer, thinner medium on the brush to apply the colour. Clove oil or aniseed oil are good; some painters use turpentine but this can produce a streaky effect.

To apply the colours to the china, dip the tip of the brush into the painting medium and then into the mixed colour. Apply the brush to the edge of the mixed paint – do not take colour from the middle of the pile or you will take up too much. It is best to transfer some of the colours you wish to use on to a separate tile. This will avoid adding more oil to the mixed paint in your palette. If you use it straight from the palette you will be adding more oil each time you load the brush with colour; eventually it will get too oily and you will have to clean all the colour off and start again.

Apply the colour in smooth, clean strokes, not too much at a time. The idea is to paint transparent washes of colour on to the china. If you use too much colour, you will find yourself pushing it around, and the end result will be a build-up of paint which you will find difficult to manipulate. Pink and purple are the two worst culprits, and these colours should be applied very sparingly. They contain gold and can sometimes be gritty; however, the better quality colours are very smooth.

When you have applied colour to the design, hold the piece up to the light to make sure it is not too oily. If it looks too shiny or runny, the paint will spread in the kiln when fired, and spoil the piece. The applied colour should be clean, smooth and fairly dry-looking.

Transfer mixed paint from the palette to a clean tile before dipping your brush into it. It is also a good idea to pour a little oil into a separate small dish.

KILNS

For me, firing china is a constant source of pleasure – I can hardly wait to see the fired pieces when I open the kiln. It is the culmination of all the previous effort as without it the work would be unfinished and impermanent. Each successive firing is a new experience and it is essential that it is understood, otherwise one's knowledge of the art of china painting is incomplete.

Firing the kiln is a process often shrouded in mystery, but it is a very simple operation when carried out correctly, and once you have done it a few times you will wonder why you ever thought it complicated. As china painters we are fortunate to have the opportunity to fire our own pieces – in the commercial potteries, pieces are fired in a separate department after the artists have finished painting them.

WHAT HAPPENS IN THE KILN

After the decoration has been applied, the painted pieces are stacked in the kiln. This is then programmed to the correct temperature, 1382–1594°F (750–850°C), depending on the type of ware and

Two conventional top-loading kilns. (Photo: courtesy of Potterycrafts)

decoration. During firing, the glaze softens and the decoration, be it a transfer or a handpainted design, fuses into the semi-molten glaze, making the design permanent.

BUYING AND INSTALLING A KILN

Kilns are the most expensive item used in china painting but they will last for years if used correctly. If you decide to buy a kiln, do not be tempted to buy one too small as you will probably want to fire a large plate or vase at some time. A firing chamber measuring approximately 11×11×15in (28×28×38cm) is a good size for your first kiln.

There is a range of small kilns on the market which are reasonably priced and can be plugged into the domestic electricity supply. Always check electrical requirements and regulations with your supplier. These should always be included in the manufacturer's instructions and should provide advice on siting the kiln and safety procedure. When you have chosen a kiln it must be correctly placed in a convenient location and, if necessary, installed by a qualified electrician. I keep my kiln in the garage.

Space must be left around the kiln to allow for proper air circulation, as good ventilation is essential. If small children have access to the room where the kiln is kept, a safety lock for the kiln door is a must.

The rules and regulations on safety should be strictly adhered to when using a kiln; these should be listed in the booklet which comes with it. If in doubt, contact your supplier. I strongly recommend an automatic control as it removes all the guesswork – it is well worth the extra expense.

TYPES OF CONTROL

Temperature control There are two types. The first is automatic, allows you to set a required temperature and will automatically switch off the power when this temperature is reached.

The second type of control holds the pre-set temperature for a time – this process is called 'soaking'. The temperature inside the kiln is measured by a thermocouple (a probe which is inserted inside the kiln).

Energy input regulator This allows you to determine the input of electricity into the kiln on a scale from 1 to 100%, regulating the rate at which the kiln heats up. Sometimes the controls are marked low, medium and high. I almost always fire my kiln on a high setting, at around 80%, and occasionally on full power, and I have rarely had any pieces break in the kiln in 25 years. The only time I use the low, medium and then high setting is when I am firing a large special piece or a large flat porcelain tile.

Electronic controllers These are very sophisticated, combining the above functions and more. They allow you to set a delayed start time, to take advantage of off-peak rates, and to set low, medium and high temperatures at desired times. These give the maximum control.

Kiln sitter If the kiln does not have an automatic controller, it is possible that it will have a device called a kiln sitter. This excellent gadget consists of a sensing rod which enables you to control the temperature with the use of a ceramic pyrometric cone. This small bar of clay is supported on metal prongs inside the kiln and placed so that the sensing rod rests on it. When the correct temperature is reached, the cone bends and triggers the sensing rod which in turn switches off the power. It is

---

PYROMETRIC CONES

You will find the following guidelines useful when using Orton cones. The figures represent optimum firing temperatures. Refer to the manufacturer's handbook for full instructions; there will be slight variations between individual kilns.

FIRING RATE :	MEDIUM 212°F (100°C) per hour	HIGH 302°F (150°C) per hour
No. 018	1303°F (706°C)	1323°F (717°C)
No. 017	1357°F (736°C)	1377°F (747°C)
No. 016	1429°F (776°C)	1458°F (792°C)

The lower the cone number, the hotter the firing temperature.

---

advisable to paint the prongs with batwash, which is a powder mixed with water, to prevent the cones sticking to the prongs. Cones have numbers on them which denote the temperature at which they will bend and melt. They are very efficient and I have had only one malfunction in the years I have used them in my small kiln.

The cones used for china and porcelain are mostly 16, 17, and 18.

It is a good idea every so often to paint batwash over the kiln's shelves (called 'bats') to remove any likelihood of china sticking to them. There are many different stilts, cranks and supports made for stacking the ware in the kiln – these items are called 'kiln furniture'.

FIRING

STACKING THE KILN

Placing the china in the kiln is called stacking. It is important that this is done correctly and therefore requires a little thought. First you must take into consideration the type of ware you are firing. If it is English bone china or soft paste porcelain the pieces must not touch, otherwise they will stick together during firing. If Japanese or hard paste porcelain is used it is possible to stack the pieces carefully on top of each other or to fire

lidded boxes with their lids on, therefore allowing more pieces to be fired at once.

The second point to consider is the onglaze colour, as different colours require different firing temperatures (see list below). Bear in mind that the hottest part of the kiln is the top. If you have a number of pieces painted in a mixture of different colours, set the kiln at 1436°F (780°C) and place pink and purple pieces, which need a slightly hotter fire, at the top. The pieces with reds should be stacked at the bottom, while lustres, gold and silver should be fired separately at a lower temperature.

If china breaks in the kiln it is usually due to a fault in the ware and not due to the person stacking the kiln, unless the stacking was done carelessly. Bone china tends to break more often than porcelain – I have never had a piece of porcelain break in the kiln. Do not allow pieces to come into contact with the elements of the kiln as they will certainly break.

ONGLAZE COLOUR AND FIRING

During the firing process, the paint burns and changes to a dirty brown colour before it fuses with the glaze. Its appearance will change many times before it eventually matures and the true onglaze colours appear. The fired colours look the same as the colours you painted but will now be under the glaze. Pink colours do change a little, usually to a prettier shade. Cadmium reds give the most trouble (see pages 11–12)

and will fade if fired too hot. There are some new cadmium reds and oranges which will take a high fire up to 1436°F (780°C). These are available from suppliers who stock colours from the USA.

If you do not fire hot enough, the colours will have a dull appearance and will not have sunk into the glaze properly. This could result in the colours not being permanent. If you fire too hot, you run the risk of distorting the colours, and if very hot the colours could burn off completely.

Sometimes during firing, 'texture' materials such as raised enamels expand or contract at a different rate to the glaze, which creates stresses. These can cause the onglaze enamel to 'pop off' or cause gold or lustres to crackle. If the enamel, or paint, 'pops off', it usually takes the underlying glaze with it, exposing the bisque underneath. It is important to take note of the kiln manufacturer's instructions when firing 'special effect' materials.

The smell from the kiln during the initial stages of firing is caused by the oily mediums burning off. These are noxious gases and should not be breathed in, so always fire the kiln in a well-ventilated area. There will be a small hole measuring $1\frac{1}{2}$ to 2in (4 to 5cm) in diameter on the top or side of the kiln. This is to allow the gases to escape during the early stages of firing and you will be provided with a bung to seal this hole at the appropriate time, when all the noxious gases have burned away and the kiln reaches approximately 752°F (400°C) (for onglaze colours). *Never* start to fire the kiln with the bung left in the hole because if the gases are not allowed to escape, your colours could become badly distorted and the kiln's elements will be damaged. Elements are expensive to replace. However, it does not matter if you forget to insert the bung during firing – it will just take a little longer for the kiln to reach temperature and it will cool down more quickly.

Do not expect miracles from your firing. If you put a badly painted piece into the kiln, you will remove a badly painted piece!

My large kiln usually takes 4 to 5 hours to reach the desired temperature, my small kiln

---

RECOMMENDED FIRING TEMPERATURES FOR ONGLAZE COLOURS

1364°F (740°C)	*Cadmium colours (bright reds, oranges)*
1328–1400°F (720–760°C)	*Gold, platinum and lustres*
1436°F (780°C)	*Majority of colours*
1472°F (800°C)	*Pinks and purples (called gold colours)*
1562°F (850°C)	*Satin metallics*

Kilns do vary and the above is a general guide.

1¹/₂ hours. When the firing is completed, the kiln should be switched off. A fully loaded kiln will take longer to fire than a part-loaded kiln.

If you do not own a kiln, your teacher or a potter may fire for you. If you have to transport pieces for firing, cover them with clingfilm and make lidded boxes secure with Blu-Tack inside their lids. Plates can be safely transported upside-down on a piece of wood and secured by elastic bands.

If you are having pieces fired for you, remember that stacking and firing the kiln is a time-consuming procedure so do not expect your china to be fired for nothing. Your teacher will have a scale of charges appropriate to the kiln used. If you are firing for someone else, be sure to point out any nicks or cracks in the china which may not have been noticed as you may be blamed for them after firing.

AFTER FIRING

It takes several hours for the kiln to cool down sufficiently for you to unload it, but when the kiln has cooled to approximately 392°F (200°C), the door may be opened *slightly* to complete cooling. Never open the kiln door while it is switched on. When cool, the china may be unloaded carefully. The coolest part of a front-loading kiln is the bottom, so unload from the bottom first.

If the fired pieces are a little rough to the touch, a very light rub with extremely fine sandpaper will give a smooth finish. However, do this only once or you will scratch the glaze. Do not use sandpaper on gold or lustres. To make a really fine sandpaper, rub two pieces together; this will take away any coarse grains and leave a fine-textured surface which can be used to smooth over the china. 'Wet and dry' sandpaper is ideal, or use the abrasive plastic side of a pot scourer.

Quite often, little black spots or blisters appear during firing. This is because the china was faulty, old or damp – yes, china can sometimes absorb water vapour. For this reason, it is not wise to fire antique pieces. Black spots usually appear on the underside or around the base of bone china. This fault can arise from the burning of the organic ingredient in the painting medium which forces carbon into any porous areas of the glaze. If this happens often, change your organic medium for a water-based one. You could also fire more slowly, allowing time for oxidization – leaving the bung out for longer than usual sometimes helps.

'Spit out' is a fault which occurs most often in earthenware, rarely in bone china, never in porcelain. After firing, the china is covered with tiny blisters, giving the appearance and feel of emery paper. This spit out is caused by water vapour penetrating the glazed ware and then being absorbed into the body. When the piece is decorated, the subsequent firing causes the water to turn to steam which builds up pressure and blows through the softened glaze. Some painters grind a small area of glaze from the base of the piece which allows the steam to escape – a carborundum stone can be used for this. When spit out occurs, it cannot successfully be rectified.

Be prepared to repeat the painting and firing process until you are happy with the result. If the paint chips during firing, it is because it has been applied too thickly: *light* applications of colour are what we are striving for. This mistake is usually only made once – it is very disappointing when it happens after spending hours painting! If the paint looks dull or rubs off after firing, it has not been fired hot enough, so fire again at a higher temperature. If fired too hot, the glaze will be very glossy and the colours distorted, leaving ridges in the glaze and the pinks with a reddish tone. A correctly fired piece will have a glossy surface, and all the colours will be clear and bright under the glaze. If you have colours which fire consistently dull at the correct temperature, you may have a colour with insufficient flux in it. Flux is an agent added to china paints to help them fuse with the glaze; it will also ensure a glossy finish after firing. To alleviate the problem, try adding 10% of flux when mixing that colour. Personally, I would throw that colour away as most colours now fire perfectly.

FIRING –
A TROUBLE-SHOOTING
GUIDE

1   Firing is easy if you follow the rules. If your teacher tells you that firing is difficult and refuses to explain the firing process – fire the teacher!

2   When installing the kiln, follow the manufacturer's instructions to ensure proper air circulation around the kiln.

3   Do *not* allow bone china pieces to touch each other in the kiln.

4   Ensure good air circulation around pieces in the kiln during firing – provide about 2 inches (5 centimetres) of space around each, no closer than 2 inches from the top of the kiln.

5   Ideally fire bone china at 1436°F (780°C) and porcelain at 1472–1562°F (800–850°C), according to the type of decoration.

6   Never let pieces touch the kiln elements.

7   Do not open the kiln door too soon after firing – allow the kiln to cool to at least 392°F (200°C). Switch off the power before opening the door.

8   If a kiln is to be wired into the mains, ensure that it is done by a qualified electrician.

9   Do not forget to leave out the bung during the initial stages of the firing to allow the oils to burn off.

10   Never stay in the same room as the kiln during firing; the oils emit noxious fumes when burning off.

11   If the noxious gases are not allowed to escape, your pieces could look dull after firing.

12   If there are children in the family, take extra care to prevent their access to the kiln.

13   Do not be alarmed when you look through the spyhole and see the inside of the kiln glowing red with heat. This is quite normal – remember 1472°F (800°C) is *very* hot.

14   If using a kiln sitter, paint the supports with batwash to prevent sticking.

15   Never touch gold after firing while the piece is still warm as you could leave a permanent finger mark.

16   If there is a power cut, no harm will be done; just fire again.

17   Your suppliers are user-friendly. If you have a query, do not be afraid to ask.

18   Opening the kiln and seeing the fired pieces is always magic – all china painters should experience it. Ask your teacher to let you open the class kiln if you do not have your own.

19   If you think that your kiln is not firing hot enough, even though you have set the correct temperature, add on 68°F (20°C) and fire again.

20   Place bone china at the bottom and porcelain at the top of the kiln if possible.

21   *Never* open the kiln door while it is switched on and never before it has cooled down sufficiently.

22   The kiln should be brushed out from time to time to keep it free from brick particles. Clean the kiln occasionally with a vacuum cleaner.

COLOUR AND DESIGN

Colour is everywhere and very easy to take for granted. However, the science of colour is extremely complex and whole articles and books are devoted to it. Technical, scientific explanations can be confusing, so I will keep mine simple and use Charles Bassett's quote from his 1920s article which sums up colour for us painters: 'Colour is the glory of nature made manifest to the eye.' I like that.

UNDERSTANDING COLOUR

There are three primary colours – red, blue and yellow – from which all other colours are made. The best way to understand colour interaction is to look at a colour wheel. I like the one illustrated overleaf, derived from an old art manual, which has been set out as a clock face. The reds and yellow intermingle to make warm, sunny colours which are psychologically cheerful. In contrast, the blues and greens are cool, subdued colours. You can see, however, that greens containing a lot of yellow become 'warmer' and purples containing a lot of blue look 'cooler'. It is important to realize, therefore, that there are 'warm' blues and greens and 'cool' reds and yellows.

The colours between the three primaries are called secondary colours and are made by mixing two primaries. By further mixing of colours, we will obtain shades such as russet and olive – these colours are known as tertiary or intermediate colours.

Complementary colours are those which lie opposite, or almost opposite, on the colour wheel. Two complementary colours mixed together in equal quantities will give a shade of grey. Two complementaries placed side by side intensify each other, but do not change their own value. Non-complementary colours seem to change when placed side by side – try it and you will see.

Trace the circle below the colour wheel and place it over the wheel. This will reveal the 'true' complementary of any one colour, plus two others which also go well with it.

Another well-known property of colour is that warm colours 'advance' and cool colours 'recede'. Thus a red flower on a cool blue background will stand out strongly, whereas a cool blue flower on a strong red background would look less dominant. Some colours are more dominant than others, for example just a tiny bit of vermilion in a painting easily becomes the most dominant hue.

HARMONY

Colour harmony can be achieved by using the colours immediately next to each other on the wheel, for example yellow, yellow-green and yellow-orange, or red, purple and violet. If you want to create a two-colour harmony just use two colours next to each other on the wheel, or the first and third of any group of three. The natural order of colours on the colour wheel, starting randomly with yellow, is: yellow; yellow-orange; orange; red-orange; red; purple; violet; blue-violet; blue; blue-green; green; yellow-green. Take any group of consecutive colours from this sequence to achieve harmony in your colour design.

Experience and practice will help you gain confidence when choosing colours. Do not be afraid of colour; try different colour harmonies and sometimes break the rules – to achieve a good contrast and impact you must apply light against dark. At exhibitions, I see plates with lovely designs spoiled because they look bland, when just a touch of rich, dark colour in the shadow areas would make the painting 'sing' and the design come alive.

*A well-balanced pattern
based on a triangular
design.*

SHADOWS

You will often need to paint shadows on to
your designs to make them more lifelike.
The main thing to remember is that warm
lights produce cold shadows (on a bright,
sunny day the shadows will be bluish), while
conversely at night in the cold moonlight the
shadows will appear a warm purplish-black.

COMPOSITION

The success of your finished design
depends to a great extent on good
composition. If the painting technique is
good but the design is poor, then you will be
disappointed with the overall result. If, like
me, you have not had any art training, you
will need to study this aspect of china

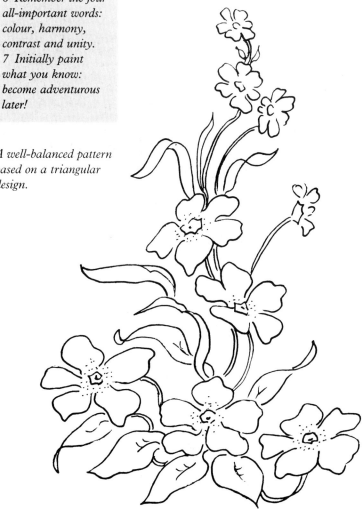

painting. There is plenty of information
available to help; most art books have a
section on composition. Initially you may
want to copy designs, but with practice you
will learn to adapt some of these to your
own individual style and this is the first step
in learning how to design for yourself.

Your design should have a focal point but
this should not totally dominate the rest of
the painting. In a flower study, the focal
flower is called 'the leading lady'. The rest
of the design is secondary and should
complement this focal point. The design
should complement the shape of the piece –
if it is small and dainty, do not paint large
flowers such as tulips or azaleas: keep the
flowers small and dainty too. Conversely, if
you are decorating a large vase, tiny flowers
would look out of place. Study the ceramics
in your local museum and art galleries to
understand these points; try browsing in
antique shops to gain inspiration.

There should be a unity within the
composition; it should not appear as a
collection of jumbled bits and pieces. I find
that the best way to achieve this unity is to
divide a plate into three. One-third will
be for the main design, one-third for
the painted, filtered background, and the
remaining third is 'negative' space. Working
to this specification, you should achieve a
unified design.

It is important to decide from which
direction the light is coming on your design
before you start to paint. For instance, if the
light is going to come from the top left of the
design, the bottom right portion will be the
shadow area. Therefore, the lighter area at
the top left should show some yellow to
suggest sunlight. Remember also to account
for reflected light from nearby objects.

Design is often subjective, but a good
design will generally please and a bad design
will be obvious to people with no eye for art,
but who know that 'something does not look
right'. To avoid producing a bad design,
always look at your piece carefully before
placing it in the kiln. You may be able to
improve it dramatically simply by adding a
touch more paint, or by changing the design
slightly.

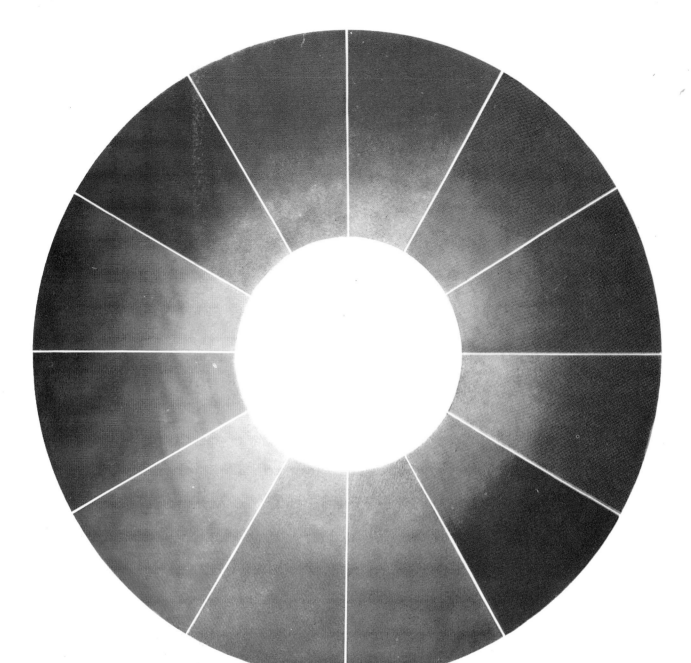

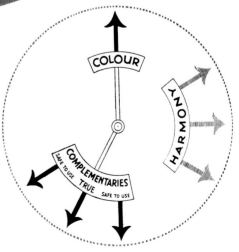

COLOUR WHEEL
Trace around the smaller wheel, and place the tracing in the centre of the larger one. This will enable you to locate the true and close complementaries of a colour. By following the 'harmony' arrows you will find those colours which can successfully be placed together.

HEALTH AND SAFETY

Before we start, a word on health and safety. *Always* observe the manufacturer's instructions on safety and bear in mind the following, based on my experience.

Some of the materials used in china painting are dangerous, but then so are bleach or aspirin if they are abused. We know how to handle these domestic items by being aware of the dangers and applying common sense in using them. It is the same with china painting materials.

- Powdered onglaze colours are toxic if inhaled; and it is essential to use a mask when mixing large quantities of powdered colour. Once the powdered colours have been mixed with the oil medium, they are safer as they cannot be inhaled, but they should *never* be introduced into the mouth by licking brushes.
- Ensure good ventilation in your work area.
- Keep your work area *clean* – if powdered colours are spilled, wet-wash the work area immediately.
- Wear suitable protective clothing and wash it regularly.
- When painting, make sure there is no loose powder on your palette – not only can you breathe it in but it will get into your painting and ruin it. Any spills should be wiped up *immediately* and the tissues disposed of.
- All containers must be properly and clearly labelled.
- Always store solvents in a safe place in well-lidded containers and keep them under lock and key if there are children in the family.
- Always store powdered colours in sealed lidded containers.
- Organic mediums and solvents have a low flash point so keep them away from naked flames and store in a cool, airy place.
- Do not eat or drink in the workshop.
- Do not smoke whilst painting – the paint particles can melt into the cigarette and be inhaled or transferred to the mouth.
- Always wash your hands after each painting session, and particularly before handling food.
- Rags and tissues used for cleaning brushes should be safely disposed of immediately at the end of your painting session.
- Do not inhale solvents under any circumstances.
- If any of your colours contain lead or cadmium, they should not be used to decorate areas of china and porcelain that will come into contact with food.
- It is important that pieces which are to come into contact with food are fired at the correct temperature. Underfired colours may allow the colour to leach out, especially if they are in contact with acids such as vinegar, wine or dishwashing detergents. There is little danger from correctly fired pieces.
- When firing in the kiln you should make sure that there is adequate ventilation and that all safety precautions are observed.
- Never stay in the room whilst the kiln is emitting noxious gases.
- The non-fire colours should never be used on pieces used for eating or drinking – use them for decorative purposes only.
- Do not sit hunched over your work for hours at a time as this can cause stiff necks, arthritis, and so on – I know; I have the joints to prove it! Get up and walk around occasionally, stretch and flex your painting hand.
- Make sure that you can see what you are painting quite clearly. I have had students who could not quite see what they were painting, producing not just poor painting but smudged lines and edges.
- The small half-spectacles designed for close work are wonderful for painting.
- Try looking at your work under a strong magnifying glass – you may be very surprised!

GOLDEN RULES FOR THE CHINA PAINTER

1   Observe the appropriate safety rules at all times.

2   Before starting to paint, decide on the direction that the light will come from. Your painting must show light, medium and dark values.

3   Apply light colours against dark for maximum contrast.

4   Do not rely too much on your traced outlines as these will disappear on firing; use your brush to establish the design.

5   Use fresh, clear colour to make your paintings 'sing'.

6   Establish good, strong highlights at the first fire stage. These are achieved by wiping out paint with a brush which has been cleaned with turpentine and wiped dry.

7   Remove unwanted colour from the china with a brush cleaned in turpentine.

8   Keep a soft, fluffy brush for blending colour.

9   Do not allow one part of the design to dominate too much.

10 Before firing always scrutinize your completed piece – can you improve it?

11 Establish the correct firing temperature for the type of ware and the colours used.

12 Sand the ware *lightly* with soft, fine abrasive paper after firing.

13 Keep your work area immaculately clean and tidy.

14 When exhibiting, always acknowledge the original painter if the design is copied, for example from a study course or a book.

15 Most important of all, have fun!

Trying Out Techniques

In this part of the book you will learn how to create a wide range of effects, from simple painted backgrounds through to exciting special effects, and the projects included in each section will develop your skills at handling the techniques. Once you have mastered the basics you can combine them with designs of your own choice, enabling you to produce beautiful painted china reflecting your own style.

BACKGROUNDS

Backgrounds can be applied before or after painting the main design, whichever you prefer. The background enhances the design as a whole and is my favourite part of the painting process – the effect of floating those subtle colours over the surface of the china is quite magical. There are several types of background which may be used to enhance the design, but whichever you choose you must pay attention to the colour balance. Try not to let one area pull your focus – hold the piece in front of a mirror and you will instantly see any areas which need attention.

Always use the largest brush that you can handle as you will never paint a good background if you use a brush that is too small. You will need flat shaders of at least ½in to 1½in (13 to 38mm), depending on the design.

SILK PADDING
BACKGROUND
Apply colour with a flat brush and then dab it smooth with a pad made by covering a ball of soft cotton wool, approximately 2in (5cm) diameter, with a piece of pure silk.

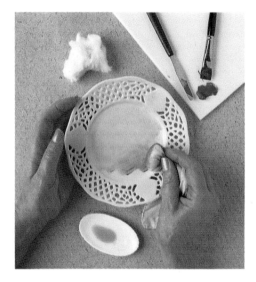

SILK PADDED BACKGROUNDS

Silk padded backgrounds produce wonderfully smooth coloured surfaces on which to paint. The silk should be very fine and soft with no visible grain as this would create marks and spoil the smooth effect. There should also be no creases in the silk, or lumps in the cotton wool. Your padded colour will be pale, as some will be absorbed by the silk in the padding process. This fired background may now be used as a basis for your design.

SPONGING
BACKGROUND
Apply colour with a flat brush. Dab it smooth with a small high-quality natural sponge. The sponge gives a more textured effect than the silk pad.

SPONGED BACKGROUND

A sponged background will appear less smooth than a silk padded one, and usually the colour will be much stronger. This type of background can be used as an edging for a design which has already been fired. It can also be used as the basis for wipe-out designs (see page 40). A variation on this theme is to use stencils and to sponge on the colours – this is particularly effective on designs for children.

An excellent technique for beginners is to collect a few leaves from the garden (oak leaves are particularly effective), and draw around them with a felt tip pen (this outline will fire off in the kiln). The leaf patterns should then be masked out with a special masking fluid used for china painting (see page 15). This is allowed to dry for about twenty minutes and when completely dry, the colours can be sponged over the entire plate. When the sponging is complete, remove the masking fluid with the point of a pen nib. It should come off easily in one piece. The leaves will be white on a coloured background and can be painted after firing. They also look very pretty outlined and veined with gold using a fine mapping pen.

If you want a really dark background, sponge and fire the piece several times until you achieve the desired effect. However, do not apply the paint too thickly or it will pop off in the firing process. This rule applies particularly when you are working on porcelain.

BRUSHED OR NATURALISTIC BACKGROUND

In my opinion, this is the most interesting background to do and is the one most commonly used for naturalistic painting. Subtle background colours are applied which complement the main design and create a sympathetic backdrop. It is an essential and invaluable technique and should be mastered as soon as possible.

You can use a silk pad to blend the colour around the edge of the china, then work on the background surrounding the main design before firing. If you find it easier, paint and fire the main design and then filter in the background colours – this is purely a matter of personal preference.

TINTED BACKGROUND

A tint is a pale, even wash of colour which is applied all over the china and fired before the main design is applied. It gives a smooth layer of colour and, if correctly applied, no areas of light or dark contrast. The tint provides a good surface for the painter to work on. A monotint is a tint of one colour only. A multitint is, of course, a tint of several colours.

To apply a tinted background, apply the colour over the entire surface with a synthetic soft flat brush – a ¹/₂in (13mm) flat shader is a good size to start with. Pad the wet paint with a silk pad until a smooth, even colour is achieved. The silk pad must be free from creases or it will spoil the tint – only fine grain, pure silk should be used. If more than one colour is used, they should be padded so that no defined edges of colour are visible. Fire tints at 1472°F (800°C) for a perfect glaze.

When a design is painted over the fired tint, any highlights that you wipe out at this stage will show the tinted colour underneath. When using a multitint, think about where the design is to be placed – for example, if you are painting pink roses, apply a pink tint where the roses will be placed.

NATURALISTIC BACKGROUND
Sketch the main design on to the china and then carefully brush the background colour around it with a flat shader brush, placing the darkest colours on the shadow side of the design. Use the 'C' stroke extensively for this background, filtering and blending the brush strokes together with a blending brush to create a light, textured effect which suggests shadows. This technique needs lots of practice. The plate above is decorated with a naturalistic background.

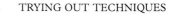

BACKGROUND FOR WIPE-OUT DESIGNS

Wipe-out flowers are a favourite technique of many china painters and are lovely to do. Apply the colours of your choice to the china keeping the deepest colour in the area where the main design will be. With a wipe-out tool or cocktail stick, mark the design into the wet background. Using a dry brush cleaned in turpentine and dried thoroughly, clean out the paint to reveal the original surface of the china.

If larger areas of colour are to be wiped out, wrap a piece of silk around your index finger and push out the design with this finger. If you prefer, you can first draw or trace the design on to the china with a very fine waterproof felt tipped pen as these guidelines will disappear after firing.

Large Tile with Wipe-out Flowers

I wiped out the design on this large porcelain tile from a wet background, using a piece of pure silk wrapped around my finger. There is no line sketch to follow for this project as the idea is to create a slightly abstract design. I painted and fired the tile three times, but if you apply plenty of colour you can probably complete it in two fires.

COLOURS USED
yellow · yellow-red · American Beauty · mauve · grey · warm yellow · chartreuse · black

BRUSHES/ EQUIPMENT
silk pad · wipe-out tool · 1in (2.5cm) flat brush · blending brush · small pointed brush

(Right) The tile after the first fire. You can see that I have created the petal edge using the wipe-out technique.

(Opposite) The finished tile. The colour has been strengthened considerably, and the flowers are much more prominent.

FIRST FIRE

❖ With a 1in (2.5cm) flat brush, apply a variety of different colours over the tile – yellow, yellow-red, American Beauty, mauve and grey.

❖ Use a wipe-out tool on the wet paint to establish roughly the position of the flowers, allowing them to overlap slightly.

❖ Tightly cover your index finger with a piece of pure silk and wipe the colour from the flowers, starting with the flowers towards the back of the design and working forwards.

❖ There will be colour left on the flowers – use this to establish shading by blending it with a soft blending brush.

❖ Paint in the centres of the flowers with warm yellow, using a small pointed brush.

❖ Fire at 1436°F (780°C).

SECOND FIRE

❖ Apply more colour to the background, making the design darker on the shadow side. The light side is where you should have applied the lighter yellow colours at the first fire stage.

❖ Roughly indicate the leaf shapes – add some chartreuse.

❖ Make the flowers darker where they are in the shadow.

❖ Fire at 1436°F (780°C).

THIRD FIRE

❖ If necessary, make the background darker to achieve an effective contrast, using American Beauty. Carefully paint detail in the flower centres with black.

PENWORK

Working on china with a fine pen is extremely versatile and can add a new dimension to your designs. Students often ask what to do with the edge of a plate – often the answer will be to pen a fine design around it. This pattern must not dominate the main design and should be applied with a very fine nib. Pen and wash is an excellent medium for china designs and can be used in exactly the same way as with watercolour technique. It is also an extremely effective way of applying oriental designs – attractive motifs can be applied to the clothing and fans of oriental figures.

The penwork must be very fine and of uniform thickness; the strokes must be smooth and not scratchy. The success of good penwork relies on two things: a fine nib and a pen medium which mixes with colour and flows easily through the nib. If either of these two is not quite right, you will not be able to achieve a good result. Students have more trouble with penwork than any other single thing in china painting. I have found that the two main reasons for this are a bad pen nib and a pen mixture which is too thick.

THE PEN NIB

The pen nib should be firm and not flexible – the mapping pens by Conté (with a recess in the barrel for safe storage of the nib when not in use) are ideal. If the pen is too flexible, the performance on the smooth china will be poor. Also, always ensure that the pen is perfectly clean before you start to write, and that the nib is not damaged.

THE PEN MIXTURE

As mentioned earlier in the book (see page 15), there are many commercial oil-based mediums available for penwork which all work well. However, the one I prefer to use with my students is the E S Outlining Oil No. 178, which is an aniseed-based medium. Mix this to an inky consistency with the onglaze colour and then apply to the china. It works perfectly every time and dries in approximately twenty minutes so that you can start adding colour to the design.

Some pen oils will not dry until they have been fired. However, whichever you choose to work with, the following points will apply.

• Mix onglaze powder with the pen medium on your tile to an inky consistency – not too thick or it will not flow through the nib.

• Check that you have mixed the colour and medium to the correct consistency by slowly writing your name without re-dipping your pen.

• The colour should be clear. If you are getting a frayed edge to the lettering you have added too much of the medium, while if the pen will not write, you need more medium.

• Always write slowly, allowing time for the inky mixture to flow through the nib. You cannot write as quickly as you would with a ball point or fountain pen.

• Hold the nib at the correct angle – it will not work if you hold the pen too upright.

• Mix the pen oil and colour on your tile occasionally, as it has a tendency to separate.

If you make up too much pen medium, you can scoop it up and put it in a small bottle. I have a bottle of pen medium ready to use and if I have any left at the end of a painting session I just add it to the bottle. Every so often I add a drop or two of turpentine to keep it thin, and before use I give the bottle a good shake to distribute the sediment of paint at the bottom. If I have a completed painting which lacks impact I add a little penwork around the design – broken strokes, not a solid black line – which works wonders. I call it 'Shaping up with the pen'. I occasionally run seminars on penwork and students bring all the pieces which need 'something doing to them but I don't know what!' Try it – you will be delighted with the result. You could also try using different colour pen mixtures.

TIPS

1 Use a good firm nib.
2 Mix the medium and powdered colour to indian ink consistency.
3 Keep the nib clean.
4 Regularly stir and mix the pen oil on the palette.
5 Penwork must be uniformly applied.
6 Before working with the pen, lightly smooth the china with fine sandpaper to prevent 'scratchiness'.
7 Change the nib regularly.
8 When tracing your design on to the china do not use the very greasy graphite paper because when you go over the design with your pen, the nib will block with loose graphite. .
9 Outlines can be penned in gold but if you decide to do this, complete the flower painting first and do the outlines last.

Materials and equipment used for penwork. The plate has been decorated with black ink and is ready for firing. Once fired, it can be brought to life with onglaze paints.

Vase with Penwork Flowers

This project takes a long time but is very enjoyable. First pen the flowers onto the china in black and then fire. If you prefer, you can pen one side of the vase first and fire it, then the other side. This makes it easier to hold the vase. Fire it as many times as you think necessary – I used seven fires. Unfortunately on the last fire a large piece fell off – but I stuck it back on and no one is any the wiser!

COLOURS USED
black · yellow · yellow-brown · malachite · sky blue · Turkish blue · Meissen blue · chartreuse · bright gold · burnishing gold

BRUSHES/ EQUIPMENT
pen · black pen oil · various brushes, including a ¹/₂in (13mm) flat

FIRST FIRE
❖ Mix a quantity of pen oil in your chosen colour; I used black for the flower design on this vase.
❖ Draw the flowers freehand onto one side of the vase – it is impossible to trace them.
❖ Fire at 1472°F (800°C).

SECOND FIRE
❖ Using the same method, draw the flowers onto the other side of the vase.
❖ Fire at 1472°F (800°C).

THIRD FIRE
❖ Using your chosen colours, paint in the flowers on one side of the vase choosing the appropriate brush.
❖ Fire at 1436°F (780°C).

FOURTH FIRE
❖ Using the same colours, paint in the flowers on the other side. It does not matter if they don't match exactly.
❖ Fire at 1436°F (780°C).

FIFTH FIRE
❖ Deepen any shading you require on the flowers.
❖ Fire at 1436°F (780°C).

SIXTH FIRE
❖ Using a ¹/₂in (13mm) flat brush, carefully paint the top and bottom of the vase with bright gold as shown in the picture of the finished vase opposite.
❖ Fire at 1382°F (750°C).

SEVENTH FIRE
❖ Now paint over the bright gold with burnishing gold.
❖ Fire at 1382°F (750°C).
❖ Burnish the gold with burnishing sand. Wash thoroughly.

Left: The vase after the second fire – a lively floral design has been penned and fired on to both sides.

Right: After the fourth fire, a first wash of colour has been fired on to the vase.

Opposite: The finished vase. The gold banding really brings the piece to life.

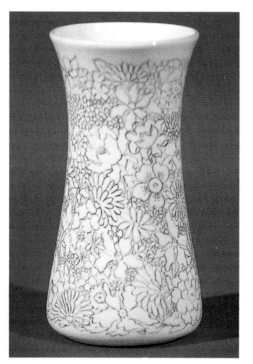

Framed Tile with Japanese Lady

This study was given to me by a student many years ago, and I have used it several times in various ways. It is not a portrait, so little detail is used on the face. The Japanese Lady plate shown in the photograph opposite uses the same design, but includes prunus blossom and a textured platinum band.

COLOURS USED
yellow-brown · yellow-red · turquoise · deepest black · cadmium red

BRUSHES/ EQUIPMENT
pen · black pen oil · ¹/₄in (6mm) flat brush and various finer brushes for detail

FIRST FIRE
❋ Trace the design onto the china and then go over the outline using a very fine mapping pen and black pen oil. Use a fast-drying pen medium (see page 15).

❋ When the outline is completely dry start filling in colour. Using a ¹/₄in (6mm) flat brush, paint the hair black. Wipe out some pale highlights (see page 40) – the hair will need more colour added at the second fire.

★ Using the ¹/₄in (6mm) flat brush, paint a wash of flesh colour lightly over the skin. Paint the design on the kimono and fan using a small pointed brush.

★ Fire at 1472°F (800°C).

SECOND FIRE
❋ Add more colour to the hair.

❋ Complete the details on the fan, hair, face, comb and kimono using the appropriate brush. Paint a wash of yellow-brown around the design with the ¹/₄in (6mm) flat brush.

❋ Fire at 1472°F (800°C).

THIRD FIRE
❋ Cadmium red was used on the collar and body of the kimono. It was painted separately with a clean brush and fired at a lower temperature.

❋ Fire at 1382°F (750°C).

LUSTRES

❊

Lustres are made from metallic oxides. The metal is held in suspension in liquid and, when fired, the heat dissipates the oxygen, destroying the organic matter in the metallic coating and leaving a hard film of lustrous metal. They are applied to the glazed surface of china to give many different effects.

Lustres were first applied to creamware and earthenware, and later to bone china. The technique was known to early Persian potters and was much used by them. During the early nineteenth century lustrework became popular with British potters for use on earthenware pottery, which was made relatively cheaply. Its immense popularity during this period was due to the ability of lustred pieces to reflect candlelight; they also took on the appearance of expensive precious metallic items but were much cheaper. Early lustrewares from this period are much sought after by antique collectors.

Lustres are available in liquid form in a variety of colours and can be used straight from the bottle. The colours all have one thing in common – their iridescence. If the bottled lustres become too thick, thin them with essence of lavender or with a special thinning agent available from china painting suppliers. Never thin liquid lustres with turpentine. Most lustres look alike in the bottle, so take care not to get them mixed up. It is a good idea to place a coloured identification label on the lid and a matching one on the bottle as a precautionary measure. Most lustres are toxic so always take care when using them. However, there are now lustres available which are non-toxic – they are usually prefixed with the letter M.

APPLYING LUSTRES

Lustres are not completely permanent. They sit on top of the glaze and will rub off gradually with wear and tear. Some lustres

Applying a mother-of-pearl lustre with a swirling motion of the brush heightens the iridescence of the finished effect.

are transparent on firing and some are opaque. You can paint a transparent lustre over an opaque one after firing and you can apply a paler coloured lustre over a darker one in the same way to obtain different effects. The last colour applied will determine the final effect. Lustres can be used alone as an all-over decoration, or reserve panels may be left white for other types of decoration, such as landscape scenes.

The liquid lustre should be applied with a soft brush or sponge on to scrupulously clean china – methylated spirit is the best cleanser to use. Finger marks must be removed from the china or they will fire as dull smudges. Once applied, the damp lustre can be padded with a fine sponge for an even finish. If a really iridescent effect is required, use a brush to swirl the lustre on the surface of the china. This technique is especially beautiful when using mother-of-pearl lustre.

When applying lustres you must work fast because some of them dry quickly. It is best to work from both sides in turn when covering a large area such as a vase. If you paint from just one side, a hard line will occur where the strokes meet. This should be avoided if possible. Also, never allow wet lustres of different colours to come into contact, unless for a special effect. Mistakes on backgrounds can sometimes be rectified by applying mother-of-pearl lustre over the fired colour, but there is always the risk that it may fire dull.

Lustres can be applied to any type of glazed ceramic. They are most effective on convex or concave shapes as their iridescence is captured beautifully by the reflected light. I prefer using lustres on English bone china as it has a soft, shiny glaze which is perfect for lustrework. If you want to be successful with this technique you must be willing to experiment. Onglaze paint applied over fired lustre is not usually successful as the lustre does not sink under the glaze and is therefore unable to absorb the onglaze colour sufficiently.

Dust is the biggest enemy when using lustres as it will leave tiny spots on the fired china where the liquid has gathered around it. The dust will burn away during firing but the marks remain as a reminder.

Keep a set of soft brushes especially for lustrework – it is not necessary to keep one for each colour provided that you always clean them with methylated spirit between each colour. Ensure that the brushes are stored in a dust-free box. Synthetic brushes are best for lustrework as they do not shed hairs. Sable brushes are too expensive for use in this kind of work.

If you want to be successful with this technique, you must be willing to buy several colours and experiment with them. Many painters give up too easily when their first attempts are not successful, but most 'failures' can be rectified in some way, and if you follow the procedures outlined here you will not go wrong.

FIRING LUSTRES

Two layers of lustre must be applied, and fired after each coat. If your lustre is not smooth, apply more and fire again. Do not apply the lustres too thickly or they will turn to powder in the kiln. The lustres are a little unpredictable – one never knows what to expect when removing them from the kiln.

LUSTRE COLOURS

OPAQUE

BRIGHT GOLD	Wonderful covering power which evens itself out during the firing.
COPPER	When fired this looks exactly like pure copper.
BRONZE	Gives a rich bronze iridescent effect.
SILVER	A warm, soft patina.
BLACK	One of my favourite rich, dark colours.

TRANSPARENT

PINK	Extremely pretty when padded with a pure silk pad then, after firing, painted with mother-of-pearl.
BLUE	Looks very delicate if padded with a soft sponge, or if painted several times becomes a deep, intense blue.
GREEN	Now available in several interesting shades – emerald is especially pretty.
VIOLET	Lovely when applied lightly. This will mix well with blue and pink lustres.
CARMINE	A rich deep red which usually needs two or three fires.
RUBY	As above, but much darker.
EMERALD	A bright green lustre.
YELLOW	This is easy to apply and mixes well with greens.
BILBERRY	A rich purple shade especially pretty if a coat of mother-of-pearl is applied after firing.
CINNAMON	A warm brown colour.
OPAL	A pale, transparent and highly iridescent shade.
MOTHER-OF-PEARL	The most widely used lustre. It is extremely beautiful painted over most other fired lustres, or on its own. It is an excellent lustre for beginners as it works well every time.

Harmonizing colours work best together – for example pinks and blues, yellows and greens, reds and mauves. If contrasting colours are applied over each other, you will often be left with a dirty grey colour.

After painting always place pieces in a dust-free area until you are ready to fire them. When loading the kiln, allow plenty of room around the pieces so that the air can circulate properly, otherwise they could appear dull after firing. Lustres need to be fired between 1328–1382°F (720–750°C). If they are over-fired they take on a dull frosted appearance. During the firing, the chimney or bung should be left open to allow the fumes to disperse. When a temperature of approximately 932°F (500°C) is reached, seal the kiln. Some lustres have a strong, unpleasant smell – always work in a well-ventilated atmosphere and wash your hands well after using them.

SPECIAL TECHNIQUES
MARBLED LUSTRES

There are two ways to achieve a marbled effect with lustres. The first is to apply the chosen lustre to the china and, when it is almost dry, to brush a special marbling fluid over it once only. This will cause the lustre to separate and create a marbled effect on the china. Fire when the piece is completely dry.

The second method is to buy the lustre already containing a marbling agent. Simply paint the liquid over the surface of the china once then leave for a few minutes. Do not go over it. It will start to separate into strange and attractive shapes – you must let it form its own shapes; you cannot coax it into shapes you want.

Different effects are achieved according to the way that you apply the marbling fluid – up and down or side to side. Marbled lustre can be used to add interest to the borders of plates, the rims of vases and much more. In landscapes such as the Mount Fuji plate pictured, it can be used to achieve stunning effects. Follow the manufacturers' instructions as they all vary a little. After firing, the marbled piece can be painted with mother-of-pearl lustre for extra iridescence.

If you wish to use the lustre around a design painted with regular onglaze colours, you must apply the onglaze colours first as they need a hotter fire than the lustres. The lustred part of the piece is therefore the last to be completed.

MASKING OUT

Lustres look pretty around reserved panels of flowers which have been protected from the lustrework. Paint the flower design first and fire. Thickly paint masking fluid over the areas you wish to reserve from the lustre and allow to dry before the lustre is applied. Then peel off the masking before firing. For complicated designs, I would suggest you use the powdered masking material as described on pages 15–16. This type of masking can be fired and is easier to use, instead of creating lots of small pieces which need to be peeled off.

LUSTRE DIPPING

This technique is wonderful to do and some exciting effects can be achieved. It takes no time at all to produce a beautiful piece for an urgently needed gift.

Put on a pair of disposable gloves, then take an old washing-up bowl or ice-cream carton, larger than the piece to be dipped, and fill with water three-quarters full. Using your palette knife or an old spoon, float a few drops of lustre on to the surface of the water. It will spread like petrol and form a thin film. Hold the china with finger and thumb, and dip or roll it into the water so that a thin coating of lustre clings to it – do this once or twice only. In parts it may appear as if there is hardly any lustre adhering to the china but, when it has been fired, you will see that there was. You can have two colours on one piece but if you mix too many together, you may not be pleased with the result.

The most effective colours for dipping are carmine, copper, black, orange, blue and gold. After firing, you can apply mother-of-pearl lustre and fire again. In my opinion, this is one of the most thrilling lustre techniques – I can hardly wait to open the kiln! If you dislike the effect after firing, you can remove the lustre with a gold eraser (a small rubber which contains some acid, available from china painting suppliers) and some elbow grease, or with a special acid solvent designed for the purpose. When you have finished *do not* throw the water from the basin down the sink or drain – dispose of it safely where it will do no damage. Most of the lustre will be left clinging to the side of the container, so wipe it out with tissues. You will not remove all of the lustre but once it has thoroughly dried, you can use the container again.

LUSTRE REPEL

Unusual effects can be achieved by applying lustre to various wet solvents and oils. First paint the china with a wash of lustre thinner or turpentine and, whilst wet, drop brush-fuls of lustre into it. Allow the lustre to run in different directions to create abstract shapes. Other oils that may be used for this technique are lavender or clove oil – each oil or solvent will produce a different effect. Try applying two or three different colours; the shapes produced can be used to simulate rocks, seaweed and other textures. These can be painted after firing with other colours, or decorated with penwork.

TEXTURING

Wet lustre can be padded with wet newspaper, clingfilm or tissue to create unusual effects.

HALO LUSTRES

Haloes are perfect circles made in the wet lustre by applying tiny droplets of different solvents. These cause the wet lustre to separate into even shapes. Spectacular effects can be obtained with practice. Halo lustre can be purchased ready-made.

TIPS WHEN USING LUSTRES

1   Keep a set of synthetic brushes, preferably nylon, especially for lustrework. Fine make-up sponges are also excellent.
2   Always thin lustres with special lustre thinners.
3   China must be 'squeaky' clean before applying lustres.
4   If several colours are to be painted on one piece do not allow the wet lustres to touch each other. Therefore plan your painting carefully and complete the piece in separate firings.
5   When firing, allow plenty of space around each piece and do not place them too close to the kiln elements. Do not seal the kiln too soon.
6   If your lustre has a dull, frosted appearance, you fired it too hot. This cannot be rectified. If there is no lustre effect at all, you applied it too thickly so re-apply thinly and fire again.
7   As lustres do not sink completely under the glaze, only use them on decorative pieces and not on those which will be in frequent use, especially plates and cups.
8   Unwanted, fired *lustre may be removed with a gold eraser or a special removal solvent. Unwanted,* unfired *lustre may be removed with methylated spirit applied with a cotton bud.*
9   A layer of mother-of-pearl over fired, coloured lustres produces a beautiful iridescent effect.
10   Never breathe in fumes from the kiln whilst lustres are firing.
11   Always work in a well-ventilated room – some lustres have an overpowering smell, especially pink.
12   You should experiment with the various lustres – this will produce hours of pleasure and surprise.
13   When using solvents to remove fired-on lustres, make sure that you treat them with respect. They contain small amounts of acid which can burn the skin so wash off immediately. Always follow manufacturers' instructions.
14   If matching pieces are required they must all be painted and fired at the same time to obtain the nearest match possible.

(Overleaf) A wide spectrum of colours and effects can be obtained using lustres; I find them great fun to paint with. Instructions for the Art Nouveau and mountain plates are given on pages 54–5.

Art Nouveau Plate

This design was adapted from an Art Nouveau brooch made in the 1920s. I decided to use onglaze colours for the wings and black lustre around the design. I also applied textured gold around the rim of the bone china plate to achieve an opulent looking finish.

COLOURS USED

black lustre · mother-of-pearl lustre · bright gold
ONGLAZE COLOURS: light flesh · crimson-brown/Pompadour · blue-violet · blue · malachite · pale turquoise · yellow-brown · yellow-red · white

BRUSHES/ EQUIPMENT

graphite paper · tracing paper · ball-point pen · mapping pen · black pen oil · I-Relief · various brushes including 1in (25mm) flat

FIRST FIRE

❖ Trace or sketch the design on to the plate.
❖ Using a mapping pen, outline the whole design with fine lines in black pen oil.
❖ Fire at 1436°F (780°C).

SECOND FIRE

❖ Apply a wash of light flesh colour to the face and crimson-brown or Pompadour to the hair using the 1in (25mm) flat brush.
❖ Paint the wings with blue-violet, blue, malachite, pale turquoise, yellow-brown and yellow-red using the 1in (25mm) flat brush.
❖ Fire at 1436°F (780°C).

THIRD FIRE

❖ Repeat the painting on the face, hair and wings to obtain rich colours, then apply I-Relief (see page 64) around the edge of the plate with a palette knife.
❖ Fire at 1436°F (780°C).

FOURTH FIRE

❖ Apply white enamel to the wings.
❖ Fire at 1418°F (770°C).

FIFTH FIRE

❖ Using the 1in (25mm) flat, apply a smooth coat of black lustre over the surface of the plate, around the main design.
❖ Fire at 1382°F (750°C).

SIXTH FIRE

❖ Apply a layer of mother-of-pearl lustre over the black lustre.
❖ Fire at 1382°F (750°C).

SEVENTH FIRE

❖ Paint the hair ornament on the head of the design with bright gold.
❖ Paint the I-Relief with bright gold.
Fire at 1400°F (760°C).

Lustred Mountain Plate

The decoration of this plate evolved during an experiment with marbled lustre and relief paste. The plate is made from English bone china.

FIRST FIRE

❀ Using the 1in (25mm) flat brush, paint the whole plate with mother-of-pearl lustre.

❀ Fire at 1400°F (760°C).

SECOND FIRE

❀ Using copper lustre, paint the mountain.

❀ Use blue marbled lustre to paint the sea. Swirl the lustre to indicate waves but do not let it come into contact with the copper lustre.

❀ Fire at 1400°F (760°C).

THIRD FIRE

❀ Using a coarse sponge, apply blue lustre to look like a large wave on the left side of the design. Paint the tree with black marbled lustre.

❀ Paint the little clouds with pale turquoise and, when dry, add fine gold penwork around them.

❀ Fire at 1400°F (760°C).

FOURTH FIRE

❀ Prepare a thin mix of raised enamel (see page 60) and pad over the big blue wave with a sponge to represent spray.

❀ Fire at 1400°F (760°C).

COLOURS USED

mother-of-pearl · lustre · copper lustre · blue marbled lustres · blue lustre · black marbled lustre · pale turquoise · gold ink · white enamel

BRUSHES/ EQUIPMENT

coarse sponge · raised enamel paste

GOLD AND PLATINUM

Gold is the icing on the cake, the final touch which adds a professional finish to your work. It is available in several forms, but the two most commonly used ones are both in liquid form – bright gold and burnishing gold. Both are made from pure gold dissolved in a synthetic resin solvent, to which bismuth is added to make the gold liquid fuse with the glaze. Bright gold is the cheaper of the two as it contains less gold. In the USA and Australia, gold is also available in little blocks or pots.

BRIGHT GOLD

Bright gold contains approximately 7 to 12 per cent gold. It comes in a liquid form which is a dark brown colour before firing. The liquid in which the gold is suspended burns off during the firing process, leaving a layer of gold on the surface of the china. Two coats must be applied, firing each one separately at 1382°F (750°C). This gold is very bright and shiny, and if used to cover too much of the china it can have a rather brassy appearance. It is therefore best used on small knobs and handles. Where a more luxurious effect is required, use burnishing gold.

BURNISHING GOLD

Burnishing gold is usually 22 carat gold and very expensive. Fortunately it can be purchased in small quantities – 5g will go a long way. Shake the bottle thoroughly before use to disperse the sediment. This gold needs two coats for a permanent finish but if you want to economize, the first coat could be painted using the cheaper bright gold. When applied it is much darker compared to liquid bright gold. After firing, the gold is dull and needs to be polished (burnished) with either a special burnishing sand or a fibreglass brush to achieve the beautiful antique-like patina.

When using the burnishing brush, it is advisable to wear rubber gloves and burnish under a running tap to wash the excess away, as the fibres can be painful if they get into the skin.

FIRING

Gold should be fired between 1328–1400°F (720–760°C). If fired too hot, the gold will crack and separate from the china. It is also important to ensure adequate ventilation in the early stages of firing, otherwise the result can be dull or blurred.

Like lustres, gold does not sink under the glaze during firing. It does fuse with the glaze, but wear and tear will cause it to rub off over time. The gold on cabinet pieces will never come off – gold can only be removed by constant use. It is possible to renew worn gold by painting and firing to make good again but *do not* attempt to do this with old or antique china as it is rarely successful.

PREPARATION FOR GOLDWORK

Keep one or two special brushes for goldwork. Gold can be decanted into specially made, lidded containers whilst working. Do not attempt to thin gold with turpentine – there are special solvents available called 'precious metal thinners'. They can also be used to thin lustres and to clean brushes. Thoroughly clean the china with methylated spirits before applying the gold, and do not put greasy fingers on the cleaned china.

APPLYING GOLD

The gold should be applied with a soft, clean brush as evenly as possible. Do not

Applying bright gold to the handles of a small vase. It is brown in appearance before firing.

This icon design, copied from a favourite Christmas card, has been decorated with flaked gold.

worry so much about the bright gold as this evens itself out on firing as it is not so viscous as burnishing gold. If the brush is 'dragging', the gold is too thick so add a few drops of the special thinners to the gold liquid and stir well. Avoid causing 'tide marks' where the strokes have dried. Work quickly to avoid this.

A band of gold can be applied around the edges of plates with the aid of a banding wheel, similar to a turntable, on which the plate has been centred. On most commercial 'limited edition' plates, the band of gold is usually the only part done by hand, taking a skilled turner just a few seconds to apply. The wheel is turned slowly and the gold is applied to the edge of the plate with a slanted brush called a 'cut liner'. This looks easy when the experts do it, but it needs a lot of practice to get a perfect band. Practise using thinned paint – do not use your expensive gold!

Unwanted *fired* gold may be removed with a specially made gold eraser. Unwanted *unfired* gold may be removed with a brush cleaned with turpentine or methylated spirit. Make sure that you remove the gold completely or you will get a purple mark after firing.

Sometimes gold can be used to disguise a badly painted colour. I used this technique on the Japanese plate on page 65. The border was uneven and I did not want to fire the plate again at a high temperature, so I painted liquid bright gold all over the plate edge. I then dripped in some solvent and allowed it to run. I fired the piece at 1382°F (750°C) – the result was very pleasing.

PLATINUM

Platinum comes in a liquid form and after firing has a beautiful soft patina which does not tarnish. It behaves in exactly the same way as gold and needs a low firing at 1400°F (760°C).

TIPS
1   Burnishing gold needs to be shaken to disperse sediments in the liquid – bright gold does not.
2   Never use turpentine to thin gold – use only special gold thinners or lavender oil.
3   Use methylated spirit to clean china prior to applying gold.
4   Gold can be applied with a fine pen.
5   On yellow raised pastework, use burnishing gold only.
6   Platinum may be mixed with gold to give a 'white gold' effect.
7   Keep a separate set of brushes for goldwork and condition them after cleaning. Soft synthetic brushes are best as they do not lose hairs.
8   If there is any turpentine on the brush used for goldwork the gold could fire dull and discoloured.
9   Gold applied too thinly will have a purple appearance after firing. To correct, apply a thicker coat and fire again.
10   If fired too hot, gold and silver will crackle and split. They should ideally be fired at 1364°F (740°C) – certainly no higher than 1400°F (760°C).
11   Do not seal the kiln until all noxious gases have burnt off.
12   Do not breathe in fumes from the solvents, nor the kiln whilst firing. Also be prepared for the dreadful smell the precious metals emit whilst firing.
13   Keep fingers away from freshly fired goldwork.

GROUNDLAYING

❀

This is a method of achieving a rich opaque colour with one firing using onglaze colours. It is the most difficult technique in china painting. To obtain this deep colour with one firing, colour must be applied thickly, but without the risk of chipping. Loose powdered colour is used for this and *a face mask must be worn at all times* to avoid inhaling the fine particles. Ideally, an extraction fan should be used.

METHOD

First, put on the face mask. Sieve the powdered colour through two layers of nylon hose so that it is very fine with no grainy lumps. For beginners, the easiest colours to use are yellows and greens; the gold colours (pinks and purples) are more difficult.

Clean the china thoroughly and paint the area to be groundlaid with a special ground-laying oil. Add a little of the sieved colour to the oil beforehand so that you can see where the oil has been applied. Then gently pad the oiled area with a silk pad until the oil is even and very dry (there should be no wet, oily patches). The pad will make a 'sucking' noise when the oil is sufficiently padded.

Using a large ball of cotton wool or a large fluffy mop brush, take up a good quantity of the sieved colour and apply it to the oiled area. Be careful not to touch the oil with the cotton wool or the brush; there must always be a good layer of powdered colour between the oiled surface and the applicator. Any remaining powder can be stored in an airtight container for future use.

When the complete area is covered, gently remove the surplus powder with a blending brush. If you have completed the procedure correctly the groundlaid area should now have the appearance of dull suede. If little areas of oil seep through, or if you can see white patches of china through the groundlaid area, you must remove the whole lot and start again otherwise it will appear patchy after firing. If correctly applied, after firing at 1436–1472°F (780–800°C) you will have a beautiful opaque, glossy groundlay. The groundlaid areas may be overpainted with gold or relief pastes. They work better on bone china than on porcelain, where they sometimes chip off.

The satin metallics (see page 65) are easier to apply than onglaze colours as they are heavier powders. They need a very hot fire of up to 1562°F (850°C) but will remain slightly above the glaze. These metallics can be painted with regular onglaze colours or decorated with penwork.

NOTE FOR TEACHERS

These loose powder techniques should never be practised by large numbers of students at the same time – even if extraction fans are in use.

TIPS

1 Always wear a face mask when using large quantities of loose onglaze powders, ideally in conjunction with an extraction fan.
2 The powder is most dangerous in its loose form – it must not be inhaled.
3 Be careful not to touch the unfired groundlay or to sneeze on it because it will mark easily. When placing the piece in the kiln beware of all sharp objects, including your fingernails, that may touch the piece. The tiniest scratch or mark will spoil it.
4 Masking fluid is used to reserve areas for other types of decoration. Simply apply as usual.
5 If the groundlay is not perfectly smooth and dry with the appearance of suede leather once you have padded it, wipe it all off and start again.
6 Fire groundlay very hot.
7 The easiest colour for beginners to use is yellow.
8 China must be squeaky clean before application.
9 Remove all surplus powder with a large soft brush.
10 Before firing, sgraffito designs may be scratched through the groundlay with a cocktail stick.
11 Remove any powder marks on the underside of your piece.
12 When groundlaying a vase, protect the inside from the loose powder with clingfilm

Green Groundlaid Vase

I am including this piece as I think that you will find its history interesting.

The vase is English bone china and I decided that a dark ground with a scene and burnished gold would look attractive. The base was separate from the body of the vase and I knew that it would not stand up in the kiln on its own as it would need a support. This would need to be a special metal rod on a base which would withstand a firing of 1562°F (800°C).

Firstly, I masked out the reserved panel and the parts to be painted with gold. I then groundlaid the dark green powder all over the vase – applying it evenly around the handles was difficult. I removed the masking fluid and fired at 1472°F (800°C). When I opened the kiln after firing it was a disaster. The metal rod support had not been strong enough and had completely melted inside the vase and formed a lump of molten metal in the bottom. The groundlay, however, was perfect. What could I do?

The only solution was to suspend the vase with special heatproof kanthal wire, fire again, and hope that the metal would melt and run out of the vase. It did, but it took a piece of the vase with it. I knew that I could only risk one more fire so I had to plan and paint the vase carefully.

First I painted the scene, applying as much colour as I dared. The handles were painted with 22 carat gold, allowing one coat to dry thoroughly before applying a second coat – all well so far. I had intended to apply a raised paste border around the centre panel but, as this would have required two more fires, it was out of the question. So I compromised and used gold transfers. This time I used the correct metal support to hold the vase and fired at 1418°F (770°C). To my relief, all was well.

I would have preferred more colour on the scene but there was little choice open to me. The base was painted and fired separately and glued on later. The broken piece was glued into place. I think all of the work was worth it and as the broken part is on the reverse side, no one knows except me and you, and I am sure that you can keep a secret!

RAISED ENAMEL AND RAISED PASTE

❊

These are two of the more decorative techniques which will add another dimension to your work. Intricate designs are made to stand out in relief from the body of the china to achieve the relief effect which was so popular on old Meissen, Sèvres and Minton pieces.

Because this work is more difficult and precise it is time-consuming, and these days is rarely seen on factory-produced pieces. It is reserved primarily for prestige pieces. I always feel that as china painters we are very lucky to have the opportunity to learn these techniques. In the china painting industry, this type of decoration would be done by specialist craftsmen, skilled in this type of work. Museums and galleries have collections of fine china and porcelain, as do stately homes, and it is these collections which give us the greatest opportunity to study these beautiful techniques at close quarters. More often than not, this relief work will be used to create patterns around a panel reserved for scenes, floral designs, birds, and so on. Good light is required for this type of work – a free-standing illuminated magnifying glass is a useful aid.

These relief materials can be purchased ready-mixed in tubes or pots but the powdered reliefs are the most frequently used and are the ones that I shall be describing. The relief powders come in two colours, white and yellow. The first thing to establish is the difference between these two powders, as this causes confusion.

MIXING RELIEF POWDERS

· RAISED ENAMEL or RELIEF ENAMEL is the white powder. It is used alone as a highlight, for example around flowers, or can be coloured with onglaze powder to make a coloured raised enamel.

· RAISED PASTE is the yellow powder and is used only as a base for burnishing gold. Both powders are mixed and fired in exactly the same way.

Traditionally these relief powders were first mixed with pure turpentine to moisten them. Fat oil was added, using turpentine as a thinning agent, to produce a soft cream consistency that would flow easily from a fine brush. This method is still used widely today. Alternatively you could use balsam of copaiba or the special commercial relief oils that are now available. The powders should be mixed with the chosen medium to a soft, workable consistency, similar to double cream. If too much medium is used the relief will flatten and possibly crack in the kiln. If not enough medium is used the pastes will not flow from the brush properly. Never use an open medium, grounding oil or olive oil to mix these relief powders as they will flatten out.

If you would like to use a coloured relief add a tiny amount of regular onglaze powder to the white relief powder and mix as usual. These colours always fire several shades darker owing to the effect of the relief powders so remember to allow for this. Keep the mixed pastes moist (breathing on them helps) as they dry quickly. The white enamel is the more versatile and tolerant of the two relief powders.

USING COMMERCIAL RELIEF OILS

I prefer using these – I mix them in the following way:

❊ Take a little relief oil on your palette knife and place it on a clean tile.
❊ Add sufficient relief powder to make a dry, crumbly mixture, then add water, a drop at a time, and mix it in until the paste resembles a soft cream.
❊ To apply the relief mixture to the china use a small fine brush with a long point.

RAISED ENAMEL

Patterns, flowers and leaves created with white raised enamel. The bottom row shows raised enamel mixed with blue onglaze colour.

Pick up a globule of the relief mixture and lay it on the china in clean, neat strokes. You can trace the shapes of the reliefwork pattern as a guide if you wish.

❖   Allow to dry thoroughly, approximately two or three hours.

❖   Fire at 1418°F (770°C).

Instead of a small, fine brush you can use other tools to apply relief pastes once they have been mixed – cocktail sticks, needle points or a palette knife.

Both raised enamel and raised paste adhere to bone china very well but will sometimes pop off when applied to porcelain. Therefore I usually add a little flux powder to the mixture to aid adhesion when it is to be applied to porcelain. Also, do not apply relief pastes over heavily applied onglaze colours on porcelain as they

will almost certainly pop off. If they do, they will remove the layer of glaze exposing the bisqueware underneath. The only way to rectify this is to apply the relief again, adding a little flux to the mixed paste.

AFTER FIRING

The white relief will look shiny after firing. It can now be painted over with lustres, onglaze colours, liquid bright gold or platinum. The yellow relief will have a matt appearance and can only be painted with burnishing gold which needs to be polished with a burnishing brush, burnishing sand or bicarbonate of soda after it has been fired. Don't be tempted to run your finger over the fired relief work – sometimes it may be sharp.

RAISED ENAMEL

Patterns, shapes and flowers painted using raised paste. In the lower half of the tile, the paste has been painted over with burnished gold after firing.

Sheila Southwell

TIPS

1   When mixing coloured onglaze powder with the white raised enamel powder, remember it will fire much darker. Beware of reds, as they will almost certainly bleach off. Turquoise, blue, pink and green are good colours.

2   If using a burnishing brush to polish gold, it is best done under a running tap as the brushes are made from fibreglass. These glass fibres on the brush break off and can get under the skin and be painful. Rubber gloves should always be worn.

3   Remember that the yellow relief powder for raised paste is used as a base for burnishing gold only. The white relief powder for raised enamel is used alone or with coloured onglaze.

4   If you paint the raised enamel with metallic colours and lustres it will resemble precious stones.

5   If the reliefwork 'pops off' repeat the process but add a little flux to the mixture.

6   To keep mixed pastes workable they must be kept moist. Place them on a small tile over a dish of hot water and let the steam do this job if you will be working for a long period. Have a small flask of hot water on your desk to keep the water hot.

7   If your raised design is complicated you can draw it with a fine pen and fire it on to the china to give you guidance, then go over the lines with the relief mixture.

8   Both raised enamel and raised paste mixtures may be diluted and drawn with a pen for fine filigree work and cobwebs.

9   Special enamel powders are now available which allow you to achieve a very high relief effect which can be built up by subsequent applications.

10   Pâte-sur-pâte is the name given to a white relief design over a fired dark background, usually comprising scenes, birds or florals. This is a specialist technique needing skill and much practice, but is exquisite when done well. The Minton factory was a leader in this technique in the eighteenth and nineteenth centuries.

11   Keep a set of brushes specially for reliefwork. They should be thoroughly cleaned and conditioned after use. Maintain a well shaped point, as with all of your brushes.

Relief Enamel Bowl

This small bowl was first groundlaid using crimson onglaze colour. The daisy design was done on a separate fire and the white relief work was done on the final fire. Bone china was used as the enamel is applied over a heavy application of colour and if porcelain is used it sometimes causes the enamel works to chip off.

If you do not wish to groundlay the border area, you can leave it white and use coloured enamel by adding about 20 per cent onglaze powder to the mixed enamel. It will fire a darker shade, so do not add too much of the onglaze powder.

FIRST FIRE

❖ Mask off the central reserved panel and groundlay the border section in crimson red, following directions on page 58.

❖ Fire at 1472°F (800°C).

SECOND FIRE

❖ Apply the black-green and chartreuse with a ¹/₂in (13mm) flat shader brush.

❖ Wipe out the small daisies with a No. 3 pointed brush.

❖ Paint in the flower centres with yellow.

❖ Fire at 1445°F (780°C).

THIRD FIRE

❖ With a small pointed No. 0 brush apply the small enamel scrolls around the edge of bowl.

❖ Paint tiny highlights around the daisy petals with the relief enamel. Don't paint highlights on every petal – just randomly here and there.

❖ Fire at 1400°F (760°C).

COLOURS USED
crimson red · black-green · chartreuse · yellow · white enamel

BRUSHES/ EQUIPMENT
¹/₂in (13mm) flat shader · No. 3 round · No. 0 pointed

SPECIAL EFFECTS

In recent years, a number of exciting special effects have been introduced to china painting which have opened up many more opportunities for experimentation. Pastes and powders, stones and sand can all be fired on to china to create all kinds of textures. These can be painted over with lustres, onglaze colours and precious metals to beautiful effect.

A whole book could be devoted to these special techniques. I have only enough room to describe a few of them in this book. The materials made by different companies have individual ingredients, so be sure to follow the manufacturers' instructions on mixing and firing.

Experiments often produce the most exciting results so have fun.

GLAZE FLAKING

This is a method of decoration where the glaze is removed from the china, thereby leaving an uneven cracked effect on the unglazed china.

Apply a powder, a paste or glass pearls to the area to be flaked. Fire at approximately 1436°F (780°C). The compound will loosen the glaze on the china so it can be easily chipped off after firing. Use a strong knife and gently lift off the glaze, which will have loosened in firing. It is usually quite easy to chip off.

When chipping off the glaze, put the piece inside a plastic bag as the chips have a tendency to fly about and can be dangerous. Also try not to use this method on the edges of porcelain pieces as they may leave a sharp edge. If they do, gently rub with a carborundum stone until smooth.

The uneven surface on the china can then be painted with either bright gold or lustres and then fired again. This technique is best used on porcelain as it can be difficult to remove the compounds from bone china as they sink into the softer glaze.

SAND DECORATION

This technique is used to obtain different textures over which gold and lustres can be painted. There are various 'grades' of sand available. Some are very coarse and some

are so fine that they provide an even, stippled appearance. Paint the recommended medium (usually balsam of copaiba) on to the china, then apply the sand over it. Fire slowly and then chip the sand off. This action will also remove the glaze, leaving an uneven surface as a basis for gold. Alternatively leave the sand on the china, paint with gold or lustre and refire. This technique gives a different effect again.

I-RELIEF

I-Relief is bought as a white powder and when mixed with balsam of copaiba oil turns into a stringy mixture. Apply it to china with a palette knife or cocktail stick. Fire slowly to 1472°F (800°C). After firing, the result will be raised lines or patterns which can be painted with gold, platinum or precious metals. The I-Relief can also be mixed with milk to obtain a more even surface. I-Relief can be used as a base for holding stones and glass chips during firing.

ENAMELS

See pages 60–1.

MATT COLOURS

These are overglaze colours to which zinc oxide has been added to give a matt effect. Mix and fire as regular onglaze colours.

LUSTRES

See pages 48–51.

HALO LUSTRE

A solvent which, when dropped into wet lustre, creates small circular haloes (circles) – see page 51.

STONES AND GLASS PIECES

When fired, small stones and pieces of opaque glass adhere permanently to china to create exciting effects. The glass will become transparent. Before firing press these ornaments into I-Relief or balsam of copaiba. If they come off during firing, they can be re-applied with instant glue. Some stones, such as river pearls, cannot be fired but are applied with glue after firing. Broken coloured glass will occasionally lose colour on firing. Collect bits of broken glass and test-fire first.

SATIN METALLIC COLOURS

Beautiful effects can be achieved with these metallic powders which come in many shades including bronze, antique silver, gold, yellow-gold. They are easy to use and make a change from platinum and gold which are much more expensive. Metallic colours make beautiful plate borders and look very attractive on small lidded boxes, giving a rich metallic appearance. Do not use metallic colours on anything other than decorative pieces as they tend to remain on the surface of the china – never use them on domestic plates and cups.

Metallic colours are heavy powders which can be disappointing when applied with an ordinary medium and brush, but which are absolutely beautiful when groundlaid. Follow the groundlaying instructions on page 58, and fire at 1562°F (850°C). For safety always wear a face mask when groundlaying. After firing, these colours can be painted over with onglaze enamels.

PETIT-POINT PASTE

This provides a very attractive decoration which gives the effect of fine needlepoint. A small piece of tulle or nylon net is stretched tightly over the china and secured. The paste is applied evenly over the net and allowed to dry completely. Then the net is removed before firing. When the piece is fired, paint a design of small flowers such as rose buds and forget-me-nots over the piece with regular china paints.

GOLD ETCHING

Traditional gold etching requires the use of ashphaltum and hydrofluoric acid – it is extremely dangerous and should not be attempted. Fortunately there are now safer etching materials, usually sold in paste or powder form.

To create your design paint the etching paste on to the china – it will eat away the glaze where it has been applied, leaving the glaze in the remaining areas intact. After firing on a layer of gold the design has a two-tone appearance where the etched part is dull and the non-etched part shiny. It is beautifully decorative.

This traditional Japanese design has a border of black which, after firing, was painted with bright gold to which turps was added.

LETTERING AND SPECIAL OCCASIONS

There are all sorts of occasions for which you can produce commemorative pieces – births, anniversaries, twenty-first birthdays, retirements, bar mitzvahs, christenings, engagements – the list is endless. If you can paint on porcelain, then you will never be at a loss for a special commemorative present. You will always have something you can paint at short notice. If you need to produce something immediately, use a transfer (decal) and finish the piece the same day. If you do use one, always try to add some handpainted work to complement the transfer design.

Take great care when writing. I have seen more commemorative pieces ruined by bad writing and spacing than by anything else. For several years I offered a firing service for china painters, firing many special occasion pieces. Some of these would be well painted but with appalling writing that was badly spaced. If you know that your writing is poor, practise the lettering until you can write neatly. Capital letters are especially difficult – I find it easier to use my normal 'joined' lettering. Write slowly – you cannot write quickly and expect it to look good.

Before starting the lettering, divide the plate into quarters and mark it with a felt pen if necessary. There are also commercially available plate dividers, printed and ready to place over the plate so that you can divide it into as many sections as required. Always mark the top and bottom of the plate and use these marks as points of reference to work from. Space your wording out carefully and when you have painted the lettering on the piece, hold it up to a mirror – this will instantly show any bad spacing. If you are unhappy with it, wipe it off and start again as many times as is necessary. Do not add too much writing on the front of the piece as it will look too commercial. A small inscription is more effective, and you can then write as much as you like on the back of the plate.

CALLIGRAPHY AND THE CHINA PAINTER

The type of writing that you choose to apply to your piece can be determined by the design. If you are good at calligraphy then this will present no problem; if, however, your writing leaves something to be desired you may find that you prefer to use your normal writing slightly modified so that it has a more decorative effect. This can be done by adding a few scrolls here and there, or by making the capitals a little more ornate. I have found it difficult to use the flat calligraphy nibs with the china painting medium and I prefer to use my normal, fine pen nib for my writing. If you want bolder letters you can draw the outlines with a fine pen nib and then fill in with a brush using your regular onglaze colour. The writing on the Christmas plate was done with my normal fine pen nib.

DECORATIVE PATTERNS

Overleaf you will find a selection of decorative patterns which can be traced from the page, and used for special occasion designs. You might like to create a wedding or christening plate, or a special mother's day cup-and-saucer design. Further ideas can of course be traced from other books, magazines and even favourite greetings cards.

Christmas Poinsettia Plate

This plate was painted using acrylic non-fire colours (see page 13). It involves both penwork (see pages 42–3) and brushwork, so is a useful project for less experienced painters. The lettering is done by diluting the paint with warm water until it flows freely from the pen nib.

METHOD

❧ Write out the words you want to include on the plate, to the correct size to suit the plate. Trace over the words, once you are happy with them. Alternatively, photocopy page 68 down to the correct size and trace from the page. As you get more experienced you could apply the lettering freehand, as I did here.

❧ Using graphite paper taped to the plate's surface, trace the floral design (overleaf) on to the plate. Make sure that you cover the graphite outline with paint, otherwise they can be difficult to remove without smudging the paint.

❧ Paint the leaves first, using spruce green and a No. 4 pointed brush.

❧ Now paint the flowers, using red and the same size brush. Start with the petals on the outside and work inwards, overlapping them.

❧ Whilst the paint is still wet, use a dry brush to take out some highlights.

❧ Now start the lettering. Water down the paint so that it is thin enough to flow easily through the nib. If it will not flow well, add a few drops more of water.

❧ Remove any pencil lines with a cotton bud.

COLOURS USED
red · spruce green

BRUSHES/
EQUIPMENT
graphite paper · tracing paper · ball point pen · mapping pen

TIPS WHEN PAINTING CELEBRATION PLATES
1 Carefully divide and mark your plate before you commence painting.
2 Do not overdo the writing on the front of the piece: a little is more effective than too much.
3 Study the piece carefully – would you want to hang it on your wall?
4 Hold the piece up to a mirror before firing to check that the writing is correctly spaced and of uniform size.
5 Presentation boxes are available for all sizes of plate – they add to the pleasure of receiving.

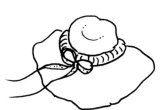

TRANSFERS

Transfer decorating is not a technique that I would recommend to the dedicated china painter but it can, and does, have its uses and you should know how it is done as part of your china painting experience.

COMMERCIAL TRANSFERS

Almost all factory-produced china is decorated with transfers. Thousands of copies of each design are printed to decorate tea sets, vases, limited edition plates – in fact, any shape of ceramic. Large numbers of pieces can be decorated quickly and fired to a standard pattern.

To create the transfers, the designs are printed onto a specially prepared paper backing. The transfer is cut out to fit the ware and soaked in water for a short time until it separates easily from the backing. It is then applied to the ceramic or chinaware, making sure that all air bubbles are pressed out using a sponge. After drying, the piece is fired at the normal onglaze temperature to make the design permanent. This is a very quick, easy procedure.

A range of commercial transfers.

PRINT AND TINT

In some factories, the outline of the design is applied with a transfer and then colour is added by hand. This type of decoration can be quite expensive – it is sometimes used on superior dinnerware.

GHOSTLINE TRANSFERS

Ghostline transfers are pale outlines of a design which are applied in exactly the same way as print and tint transfers. The colours are then painted in by hand. These designs can be very pleasing.

MAKING YOUR OWN TRANSFERS

If you have a design that you wish to repeat several times, or some lettering to apply to an awkward shape (the inside of a cup, for example), it is quite easy to make your own transfers. A special shiny paper can be purchased for this purpose. Apply your design to it by hand using a fast-drying medium such as fat oil. A pen may be used provided that you do not scratch too deeply with the nib. Allow the design to dry completely.

A plastic coating (called 'Covercoat') is applied over the dried design and smoothed over with a stiff card, taking care not to disturb the design. It is very important to go over the design with the Covercoat once only or you will pull off the paint. This technique may need some practice. Allow the Covercoat to dry completely and then your transfer can be cut out and used as described above. It is possible to use gold but make sure that it is absolutely dry.

There are companies which will make transfers from your original design quite cheaply. If your design is less than perfect after firing, it is possible to touch it up with your regular china paints.

TRANSFER SHEETS

Coloured sheets of transfer paper are available for you to create abstract shapes – just cut them out and apply as for commercial transfers. It's fun to experiment with these, and the sheets come in many opaque colours.

HANDPAINTED OR TRANSFER?

Part of my profession is as a restorer of ceramics and often, when pieces are brought to me for repair, I am asked whether they are handpainted. Sometimes it is difficult to tell without the use of a magnifying glass; however, there are some obvious differences.

If the piece has a border design or a design around a reserved panel (a panel left for special decoration) which is very regular and perfectly spaced with scrolls or dots of the same size, then it is usually transfer printed. Another way to tell is by looking at a flat area of colour, for example on a garment or in skin tone, and if you can see hundreds of tiny dots or marks close together, like dots on a television screen, these are usually a sign of silk screen or lithograph printing. Figurines usually have some handpainting, if only on the face. Of course, three-dimensional pieces such as birds and animals are painted by hand as it is impossible to put a flat transfer onto a three-dimensional object. Some figures are painted with an airbrush. Almost all 'limited edition' plates are transfer decorated with only the gold border applied by hand.

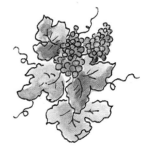

Floral Themes

Flowers are the most popular decorations for china, and they are a good first choice for beginners. The following projects allow you to try out some simple designs, following the straightforward patterns and step-by-step advice. You will soon find that flowers are both easy and enjoyable to paint.

A collection of violet and viola designs. This pretty flower is especially suitable for small and delicate pieces. (See pages 82–85.)

LEAVES

O ne of the most important parts of a flower design is the leaves. Such is their importance, they can make or ruin the most carefully painted design.

The leaves should not be overworked and should be painted in as few strokes as possible. To achieve a good contrasting effect in the design, wipe out some strong highlights before the first firing. Do not despair over awkward shaped leaves such as holly or oak. Simply paint one broad brush stroke, then wipe out the shape using a wipe-out tool and remove any excess colour with a clean brush or cotton bud.

If too many colours are introduced the design can look overworked and fussy. On the other hand, do not make the mistake of painting all the leaves the same colour as this makes a boring overall effect. Therefore, make some of the leaves darker than others, particularly the underneath ones. The leaves catching the light will be the ones which are palest. Paint the leaves a warm yellow-green for the first fire – then add any extra colour or shading at the next fire.

For an autumn study, paint the leaves with tones of yellow for the first fire, then overpaint in green.

Leaves are a very important part of a completed design and need special attention. They are not always green and they are not the same tone all over. Light and shade must be established on the first fire – remember, some leaf edges will be folded back. If I am designing a piece with just leaves in different shades of green I often use some platinum, as the combination of green and silver colours look well together.

1 Plum leaves sometimes have a yellow bloom on them.

2 & 3 The vine and oak leaves are bright with autumn colouring – paint your brush strokes in towards the centre and shape the edges with a clean, pointed brush.

4 Paint tulip leaves with long strokes.

5 Rose leaves grow in threes and fives.

6 When painting cyclamen be aware that rounded leaves often have a mauve tint.

7 The white poplar has a silver green leaf.

8 A heart-shaped leaf similar to a violet leaf. Paint strokes in towards the central vein.

SPRING

❅

When I think of spring my thoughts turn to hedges of catkins, lanes dotted with violets and primroses, and fields vibrant with ladysmocks and cowslips. The young green leaves impart a feeling of renewed life. As painters, we can't wait to capture these gentle, delicate flowers on our china and porcelain, and the pretty shapes of china now available are perfect for spring flower designs.

When painting these flowers, keep the designs fairly simple and the colours delicate – too little is better than too much. To capture the essence of spring, I have chosen tulips, daffodils, violets, primroses and bluebells. Have fun painting them!

PROJECT . . . . *Spring Flower Plaque*

The flowers are completed first. The background scene is lightly suggested and is painted on the last fire.

COLOURS USED
grey-green · brown-green · mauve · leaf green · dark green · chestnut brown · yellow-brown · deep blue

BRUSHES/ EQUIPMENT
graphite paper · tracing paper · ball point pen · small flat brush · ¹/₂in (13mm) flat brush · various other brushes

FIRST FIRE
❉ Sketch or trace the design on to a tile. Using a small flat shader, paint the primrose leaves with a pale wash of grey-green, then wipe out the centre veins with a wipe-out tool or a brush.
❉ Paint the violet leaves with brown-green, keeping the colour quite pale. With a soft brush, gently blend the colour towards the centre vein of the leaves. Wipe out one or two highlights and the turnback on the right leaf.
❉ With primrose yellow, paint the primroses. Wipe out some sharp highlights, especially where one flower overlaps another. Paint the buds with grey-green and add the stalks, using the same grey-green and a fine brush.
❉ Lightly apply a wash of pale mauve over the violets and paint their yellow centres.
❉ Add a dot of leaf green to the centre of the primroses.
❉ Paint the bluebell leaves with dark green, then the bluebell stalks with the same colour. Then paint the bluebells in deep blue. Wipe out the highlights on the side of each 'bell'.
❉ With a ¹/₂in (13mm) shader, apply a

textured wash of brown-green around the base of the design.
❉ Fire at 1436°F (780°C).

SECOND FIRE
❉ Using a ¹/₂in (13mm) flat shader, add more textured strokes around the design using chestnut brown, brown-green, yellow-brown and dark green. Then add more depth of colour to the parts of the leaves which are in shadow, where one overlaps another, and under any turn-backs.
❉ Paint the violets with a slightly deeper colour by adding some deep blue to the original pale mauve colour, remembering to maintain the highlights.
❉ Add a little more shading to the primroses with grey-green (bear in mind that they are a pale flower), then paint in the centre as illustrated.
❉ Add more colour to the bluebells, maintaining the highlights.
❉ Fire at 1436°F (780°C).

THIRD FIRE
❉ Lightly wash in a pale landscape behind the design to suggest a scene.
❉ Fire at 1436°F (780°C).

PAINTING PRIMROSES

1 The extreme centre is made up of little yellow-green buttons, surrounded by an area of deep yellow.

2 Petals have a dip in the outer edge and are palest lemon. Each flower has five petals.

3 Leaves are large and crinkly with a widening central vein, and grow straight out of the ground from a little root.

4 The deep yellow centre is pointed in five parts.

5 Calyx showing half-open floret.

6 Calyx showing half-closed floret.

7 Sometimes the flower stems are very short allowing only the flower to be seen.

(Overleaf) Spring flowers make bright and cheerful designs. Here are three for you to try.

PROJECT . . . .

Tulip and Daffodil Plate

Painting a detailed background around lots of flowers and leaves is difficult for a beginner, so it is sometimes easier to leave the background white, as in this project. This design would make an ideal golden wedding study.

COLOURS USED
chartreuse · pale blue-green · pale red-brown · Albert yellow · pale green · ivory · yellow-brown · yellow-red · leaf green · Limoges yellow/ golden yellow and white · bright gold

BRUSHES/ EQUIPMENT
graphite paper · tracing paper · ball point pen · flat ¹/₄in (6mm) brush · pointed brush · various other brushes

FIRST FIRE

❋ Trace or sketch the design on to the china.

❋ Paint the daffodil leaves chartreuse and the tulip leaves pale blue-green with a flat ¹/₄in (6mm) brush.

❋ Using a pointed brush, paint the stems of the flowers pale red-brown.

❋ Pick up the flat brush and lightly paint the daffodil flowers with Albert yellow and their centres with yellow-brown, painting deeper colours as you work into the flowers' trumpets.

❋ Wipe out the centres of the daffodils with a clean brush or wipe-out tool, and then paint with very pale green.

❋ Paint the tulip flowers with ivory, and blend in a little pale yellow-red – feather the strokes so that the colour appears very pale at this stage. If mixing the yellow-red

1   *2*   *3*   *4*

5   *6*

7   *8*

PAINTING TULIPS

(1–3) Start with the tulip centres. Paint the outer petals very pale. Gradually build up shading, and wipe out some highlights.
(4) Leaves: Use a few long, flowing strokes to paint the leaves, rather than short, fussy ones. Add a little shading and highlighting.

PAINTING DAFFODILS

(5–7) Start with the centre of the trumpet, then paint the outside trumpet. Fit the petals around it, making them darker near the centre.
(8) Leaves: Paint the leaves with long, flowing strokes.

yourself, make sure that the yellow and red are compatible – do *not* use a cadmium red or yellow.

❋   Fire at 1436°F (780°C).

SECOND FIRE

❋   Using the flat brush, apply some deeper green here and there to the leaves to give them a zing.

❋   Shade the daffodils with a deeper yellow (a mix of yellow-brown and Limoges yellow) keeping some sharp highlights visible, and make their stems a little darker.

❋   The tulip flowers should now be

shaded with Limoges yellow if you have it – if not, use a mix of golden yellow and white.

❋   Using yellow-red and a small brush, shade up the tulip petals.

❋   I padded an edge of yellow-brown around the fancy plate. This can be done using either a silk pad or a sponge (see page 38).

❋   Fire at 1436°F (780°C).

THIRD FIRE

❋   Add some gold to the border design, but this is optional.

❋   Fire at 1400°F (760°C).

Violets

The violet is an extremely well loved flower and a favourite subject of the china painter. It is often wiped out of a wet background. The china may be given a delicately tinted background and fired before attempting to paint the design. If you use this method paint the background in very pale violet, blues, pinks, greens and yellows – all these colours will look good with violets. Keep the colours palest where you intend to place the flowers. Pad the background with silk to get a smooth tint.

PROJECT . . . .

COLOURS USED
blue-violet · moss green · lemon-yellow · mauve · black · gold/platinum

BRUSHES/ EQUIPMENT
graphite paper · tracing paper · ball point pen · No.3 pointed brush · various other brushes

Violet and Viola Coffee Cups and Saucers

Matching cups and saucers are not only pretty but useful too – and they are shapes which beginners can cope with easily. Designs should be fresh and pretty, not too overpowering for the delicate shapes. All these pieces can be completed in two firings.

FIRST FIRE
❂ Using graphite paper, trace the design on to the china.
❂ With a No.3 pointed brush, paint the violets on the cup and saucer blue-violet.
❂ Using the same brush, paint the leaves with moss green and the violet centres with lemon.
❂ Using the No.3 pointed brush, paint the violas with lemon-yellow and mauve, their central 'whiskers' with black, and the leaves with moss green.
❂ Fire at 1436°F (780°C).

SECOND FIRE
❂ Paint the cup handles with gold or platinum, using a clean brush.
❂ Fire at 1364°F (740°C).

PROJECT . . . .

COLOURS USED
pink · yellow · violet · soft turquoise · blue-violet · chartreuse

BRUSHES/ EQUIPMENT
graphite paper · tracing paper · ball point pen · 1/2in (13mm) flat shader brush · various brushes, including a small pointed brush

Violet Tray

This rectangular tray is made of porcelain. I felt that a naturalistic background would complement the violets beautifully. The tray was completed in two fires, the scrolls being added on the second fire.

FIRST FIRE
❂ Sketch or trace the design on to the porcelain.
❂ With a 1/2in (13mm) flat brush, paint the background around the design, making it darker on the shadow side. For this background use pink, yellow, violet and soft turquoise.
❂ Wash a small pointed brush in turpentine and dry it thoroughly, then use it to clean any unwanted colour from the flowers and leaves.
❂ With a No.3 pointed brush, paint a wash of blue-violet on the flowers and a wash of chartreuse on the leaves.
❂ With a clean brush, gently take out some highlights on the flowers and leaves.
❂ Fire at 1472°F (800°C).

SECOND FIRE
❂ Deepen the background colours around the flower design.
❂ Add a little more colour to the violets and leaves, paint the violet centres with yellow, then paint the stems using a fine brush.
❂ Add the scrolls if required with a pen and blue-violet pen oil.
❂ Fire at 1436°F (780°C).

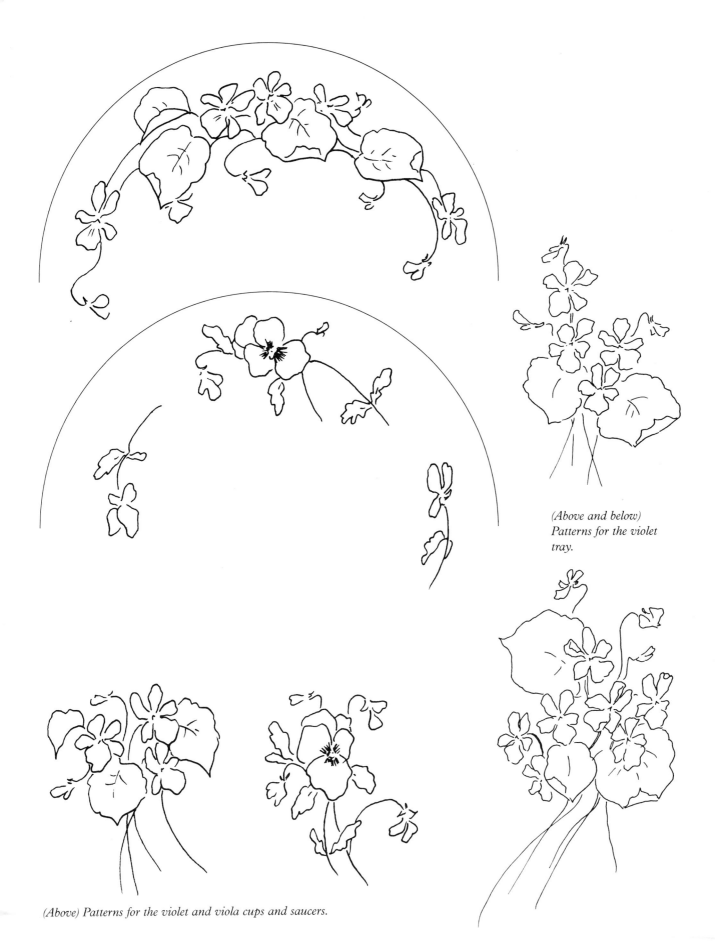

(Above and below)
Patterns for the violet
tray.

(Above) Patterns for the violet and viola cups and saucers.

Miniature Tea Set with Violets

This little tea set is made of English bone china and took three fires to complete. It was decorated with platinum – for details of how to apply platinum, see page 57.

COLOURS USED
deep blue-violet ·
chartreuse · shading
green · yellow ·
platinum

BRUSHES/
EQUIPMENT
graphite paper ·
tracing paper ·
ball point pen ·
No.2 pointed brush

FIRST FIRE
❀ Sketch or trace the design on to the china.

❀ Using the No.2 pointed brush, paint the violets with deep blue-violet.

❀ Paint the leaves with chartreuse and shading green.

❀ Paint the centres with yellow.

❀ Fire at 1436°F (780°C).

SECOND FIRE
❀ Using a clean brush, apply the platinum to the handles and knob.

❀ Fire at 1382°F (750°C).

THIRD FIRE
❀ Apply a second coat of platinum.

❀ Fire at 1382°F (750°C).

MINIATURE TEA SET VIOLETS

Here are some of the violets I have used on the miniature tea set pictured on pages 72–3. You can trace the designs from here, adapting them as you wish to suit your taste and the shape of the china. Remember to use the larger patterns on the large pieces (such as the tea-pot body and tea cup), and the smaller single flowers on smaller pieces (such as lids and saucer edges).

(Right) Scrolls used on the violet tray, page 82.

1

2

3

4

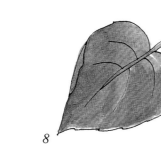

5

6

7

8

9

*1 Upside-down 'v'
forms the centre of the
flower.
2 Paint the larger
bottom leaf first, then
the two top 'ears'.
3 The remaining two
petals are painted next,
one each side of the
flower.
4 Stems should be very
delicate and wavy.
These flowers are only
part-open, seen from the
side.
5 When painting a
group of flowers, paint
the flower behind in a
darker hue, then add
the main flower.
6 Here, the balance of
the design is improved
by adding another
darker violet to the right
of the main flower.
7 A simple violet leaf
painted with a flat
wash.
8 A violet leaf with a
turned back edge.
9 Here, a flower has
been wiped out of the
leaf before being
painted.*

SUMMER

❄

'Summer' – what a wonderful sensation the word conjures up. Lazy, warm days heady with the sound of bees in the honeysuckle, long evenings when we are loathe to go indoors, and a myriad of garden flowers flooding the borders with colour all bring to mind glorious summer months. Summer is the time to sit outdoors and sketch these flowers ready to paint later. I like to take one flower and sketch it in detail, from all angles, including the leaves, bud and stem. I then do a watercolour painting of the flower, and file it away until needed. I have chosen daisies, buttercups, poppies and of course the rose from amongst the abundance of summer flowers.

PROJECT . . . .  *Butterfly and Buttercup Plate*

Bugs, beetles, moths and butterflies – what would we do without them in ceramics decorations? For over 200 years these little insects have been used to cover up tiny flaws in the surface of the ware. Yes, many of these tiny creatures painted on Meissen and Sèvres china were there to serve a purpose. Often, tiny imperfections appeared in the glaze, which if left uncovered, would mar the piece. Therefore a small beetle, ladybird or moth would be painted over the flaw to hide it and become part of the intended design.

This is an easy study for a beginner as the background is left as white. I cheated with the plate edge as it was already decorated when I bought it. This project takes just one fire.

COLOURS USED
malachite blue · dark turquoise · golden yellow · yellow-brown · light green · dark green · black

BRUSHES/ EQUIPMENT
graphite paper · tracing paper · ball point pen · mapping pen · black pen oil · No.3 pointed brush · small square shader brush · various other brushes

FIRST FIRE

❖ Sketch or trace the design on to the china.

❖ Using a fine mapping pen, outline the whole design in a pale black colour using fast-drying pen oil.

❖ Allow this to dry and then paint the flowers, leaves and butterfly, using a No.3 pointed brush for the butterfly and a small square shader for the buttercups.

❖ Fire at 1436°F (780°C).

This is the basic design used for the plate opposite. You can see that I made some slight alterations, and used different colours for the butterfly.

Daisies

Without doubt, the daisy is one of the most popular flowers to be painted on china and porcelain. Daisies come in all shapes and sizes and can be painted directly on to the china or wiped out of a wet background. They are a particularly good subject for beginners to paint once the basic brush strokes have been mastered.

Each petal should be formed with one clean stroke using the correct size of brush. Do not be tempted to crowd the china with daisy flowers – often just a few simple sprays will be far more effective than lots of fussy flowers. The leaves can be used to fill any empty spaces left in the design. On small dishes and boxes I wipe out the daisies from a dark background and quite often do not put any leaves in at all. If the piece is too pale when fired, outline the daisies with a pen using a fine broken line – a solid line will destroy their delicate effect.

In the following daisy project, I have shown several designs for you to try. Experiment with different sized brushes and have fun.

PROJECT . . . . Daisy Tile

This large tile called for a bold design and Marguerite-type daisies were decided on. They were wiped out of wet background colours.

COLOURS USED
pink · yellow-brown · baby blue · turquoise · dark green · pale green · black

BRUSHES/ EQUIPMENT
1in (25mm) tinting brush · No. 4 pointed brush · graphite paper · tracing paper · ball point pen

FIRST FIRE

❖ Transfer the design to the china using graphite paper.

❖ Using a 1in (25mm) tinting brush, apply a wash of the following colours all over the tile, the darkest colours being placed where the largest area of design is to be: pink, yellow-brown, baby blue, turquoise, dark green.

❖ With a wipe-out tool mark where the ten flower centres are to be. Only two flowers are overlapping; most of the flowers stand alone and are easy to wipe out.

❖ Starting with the top flower, using a No. 4 pointed brush, wipe the daisies out of the wet background. Make the flower under the overlapping flower slightly darker because it is in shadow.

❖ Paint the flower centres with yellow: wipe out a few leaves.

❖ Fire at 1472°F (800°C).

SECOND FIRE

❖ Apply a little textured background colour around the daisies with some green and turquoise paint mixed together.

❖ Wipe out any colour which has accidentally been painted over the daisies.

❖ Paint the leaves with pale green. Paint just a little green shading on some of the petals to suggest shadows. Paint the stems with green – not too heavy.

❖ Shade the flower centres with yellow-brown. With a fine brush paint stamens with black.

❖ Fire at 1445°F (780°C).

THIRD FIRE

❖ Adjust any background colours as needed.

❖ Fire at 1445°F (780°C).

(Opposite) Daisies are easy to paint and give delightful results on a wide variety of items.

PAINTING DAISIES

(Opposite) Very different effects can be obtained simply by choosing a different brush. In each case, the petals should be painted toward the centre point.
(Top row) Painted with a rigger brush.
(Second row) Painted with a No.2 pointed sable brush.
(Third row) Painted with a No.4 pointed sable brush.
(Fourth row) Painted with a $^3/_8$in (9mm) square shader. Stronger shadows have been added to these flowers.

TIPS
1 Daisy petals radiate from one central point and must be painted with an inward stroke, towards the centre.
2 Paint the centres with a sharp colour for maximum impact.
3 Paint each petal with one clean stroke.

Roses

The rose is the most popular flower amongst china painters, who never tire of trying to capture its elusive charm. Many different china painting factories have, over the years, developed a distinctive and recognizable style of rose painting which is particular to themselves – Meissen, Sèvres and Derby, for instance. The colours and shapes of the rose in its natural form are innumerable; add to this variety and an exquisite perfume, and surely the rose becomes the queen of all flowers.

Capturing this beauty on china is easier if you follow a few simple guidelines. Over the next few pages I will show you how to paint a simple rose, which can be adapted and added to as you become more profieient. I have also included other finished pieces to give you further ideas and inspiration. Forming the petal edges gives the most trouble but is easier in this medium than most others and can be done using either a fine wipe-out tool or a flat, chisel-shaped brush. While you are learning, paint your rose on to a tile and keep painting and wiping off until you get the 'feel' for the flower.

Two pretty rose-decorated boxes in different styles.

PAINTING A BASIC ROSE

The first two rows show the order in which to paint a rose. This is done in the following order: (1) paint the throat of the rose; (2) paint the bowl; (3) and (4) fit the outer petals around the bowl. This should be done using a flat-edged brush. The stroke is shown clearly on the top right. The third row shows how to paint leaves. Flat strokes should be practised first; these are used to fill in shapes. Next practise the comma stroke – two large commas make up a full leaf. 'C' strokes can also be used to paint leaves.

PROJECT . . . .

Cream Rose Plate with Pierced Edge

This plate invited a design which reflected the delicacy of its pierced edge. The cream rose is one of my favourites, and I created this design from studies done in my own garden. The three-rose group works well, I think.

COLOURS USED
chartreuse · pale lemon · yellow · dark brown · moss green · yellow-brown · soft turquoise

BRUSHES/ EQUIPMENT
graphite paper · tracing paper · ball-point pen · wipe-out tool · ¹/₂in (13mm) flat shader brush · 00 pointed brush · various other brushes

TIPS
1   Be prepared to paint on and wipe off until it is correct.
2   The leaves usually grow in groups of three and five, but you can use some artistic licence to suit your design.
3   Cut-out petals are made using a flat brush with a sharp edge.
4   Paint the throat of the rose first, then the bowl. Fit the outer petals around that.
5   Maintain plenty of highlights.

FIRST FIRE

❋   Sketch or trace the design on to the plate. Do not add too much detail – you only need to convey the basic shapes.

❋   Starting with the leaves further from you, paint on a wash of chartreuse using the ¹/₂in (13mm) flat shader. No veins should be painted on at this stage.

❋   Paint a wash of pale lemon on to the flowers using the same brush, making the throat of the rose a deeper tone by using a little yellow-brown.

❋   Paint some petals folding over, making sharp highlights where one flower or leaf overlaps another so that each element is sharply defined and in the correct perspective.

❋   If you feel confident, add a little colour – green, soft turquoise and yellow – around the design.

❀ Cut out some petal edges using a wipe-out tool or flat brush.

❀ Fire at 1472°F (800°C).

SECOND FIRE

❀ Darken the background in the shadiest areas using some yellow-brown and dark brown.

❀ Using the ½in (13mm) flat, gently filter some lighter colour around the whole design. Paint some yellow in the lightest areas.

❀ With a darker green, paint some shading on to the leaves and suggest one or two leaf veins in brown.

❀ Paint the underneath of the rose in yellow-brown in the very darkest areas, and more yellow on the petals where needed.

❀ Fire at 1436°F (780°C).

THIRD FIRE

❀ Add any further shading to the background and flowers.

❀ Paint the plate edge with deep brown.

❀ Fire at 1436°F (780°C).

(Overleaf) Roses look wonderful on almost any type of object. Try imitating your favourite garden rose, matching its colour and form.

Poppies

Poppies are always a joy to paint. Their stunning colour contrasts well with the white of the china, and they are in fact quite simple to do. Their exuberant appearance makes them especially suited to medium or large size objects.

Below I have chosen to demonstrate a painted plaque, but you might like to try the design on a plate or large vase, for example. On page 101 is a coffee pot I painted with a poppy design. As you can see, the poppy is a very adaptable and successful design.

PROJECT . . . . *Framed Poppy Plaque*

Poppies are always a joy to paint. I painted the piece shown below in a fairly free style on a large porcelain tile (12×14in/30.5×35.5cm), using a 1in (25mm) and ¹/₂in (13mm) flat shader brush. As you will see, the design entailed using yellow and red paints together. Make sure that these are compatible and that you have not chosen cadmium colours as they will not fire successfully (see page 11-12).

FIRST FIRE

❖ Sketch or trace the poppy plaque design onto the tile.

❖ Using the 1in (25mm) flat brush, paint the background colours around the design, with a yellow area in the top left-hand corner to indicate the direction of light. Use shades of yellow, green and turquoise.

❖ Paint the leaves with chartreuse and grey-green, then the flowers with yellow-red and shade with yellow. Blend the colours with a fluffy soft brush so that there are no hard edges showing.

❖ Paint the buds and stems, then the centres, with grey-green – do not apply any black on this fire.

❖ Wipe out highlights on the petals.

❖ Fire at 1436°F (780°C).

SECOND FIRE

❖ Adjust any background colours and make the shadow side of the design darker by applying a mixture of purple and shading green.

❖ If the flowers need a 'zing', add some more yellow-red and add any shadows to the flower underneath with Pompadour red.

❖ Paint and shade the leaves and stems with shading green and, while they are still wet, pull out the little fluffy hairs on the stems and buds using a very fine brush. Paint a touch of red inside the bud.

❖ Using the deepest black and a rigger brush, paint the dark centres of the flowers using a full load of colour – but be careful not to apply so much that it will run during firing.

❖ Using a cocktail stick, pull some fine lines outwards from their centres.

❖ Fire at 1436°F (780°C).

COLOURS USED

chartreuse · grey-green · yellow-red · yellow · purple · shading green · black · Pompadour red · soft turquoise

BRUSHES/ EQUIPMENT

graphite paper · tracing paper · ball point pen · rigger brush · ½in (13mm) flat brush · 1in (25mm) flat brush · various other brushes

*Poppies can be painted singly or in groups.
Their strength lies in their vibrant colour, so try
to match the brilliance of colour illustrated here.*

TIPS
1   Use compatible
reds and yellows –
avoid cadmium
colours.
2   The black centres
should provide a
sharp contrast so
paint them the
deepest purple black.
3   Hairs painted on
the stems and buds
should not be too
prominent.

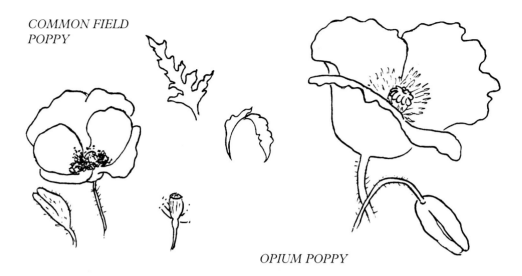

*COMMON FIELD
POPPY*

OPIUM POPPY

*(Below) Poppies on a
coffee pot.*

Summer Fruit

Painting fruit on china and porcelain has always been popular. Here are some of the soft summer fruits for you to try. Always keep some good highlights to give a spherical, plump appearance. There will also be an area of reflected light from the surrounding areas. Fruits with a smooth, dark skin will show some blue or turquoise in their make-up.

COLOURS USED
yellow · yellow-red · green · black · pine

BRUSHES/ EQUIPMENT
wipe-out tool · pen · black pen oil · /4in (6mm) flat brush · blending brush

What could be nicer to paint than luscious summer fruits? Fresh colours must be used for this, as muddy colours will make the fruit look unappetizing. Fruits should be plump with plenty of highlights to suggest roundness. The fruit is darker on the shadow side but there will be an area of reflected light on this side too. To achieve the impression of bloom on fruits such as plums and peaches, some turquoise colour is painted on the portion showing the most light – do this before the first fire.

1

2

3

FIRST FIRE

❀ Sketch or trace on the design.

❀ Paint the leaves with light green, using a ¼in (6mm) flat brush.

❀ Next paint the strawberries. Apply a little yellow in the lightest areas, then add some yellow-red, blending the two colours together with a soft brush.

❀ With the wipe-out tool, take out some small areas where the seeds are to be painted.

❀ Paint the stems green.

❀ Draw in the little flowers with a pen.

❀ Fire at 1436°F (780°C).

SECOND FIRE

❀ Add more shading to the leaves.

❀ Paint some more yellow-red on the shadow side of the berries.

❀ Mix a little black and green, and use this to indicate a shadow on one side of the wipe-out marks made for the first fire. Paint in the tiny seeds.

❀ Paint a wash of pink here and there on the flowers, and paint in the flower centres with pale yellow. Pen in the flower stamens with tiny dots.

❀ Add the penwork around the piece, using any colour you choose.

❀ Fire at 1436°F (780°C).

6

1 Use pink, yellow and a little turquoise to suggest bloom on the skin of this peach. Apply brush strokes in a circular motion.

2 The gooseberries were painted with chartreuse darkened with a little grey. Pull out the hairs on the berries using a very fine brush and wet paint.

3 For figs, use light green as the basic colour then shade up with crimson red.

4 Paint cherries first with yellow on the lightest areas, then blend in yellow-red, keeping a strong highlight.

5 Paint blueberries with blue-black and then wipe out strong highlights.

6 Use orange to paint this apple, then fire. After firing shade the fruit with a deep pink-red colour. Try to keep a strong area of light.

4

5   Sheila Southwell

AUTUMN

❋

Autumn is my favourite season. The thought of winter days to come makes autumn precious, and the remaining flowers which we may have taken for granted in their summer abundance suddenly take on greater importance.

How nostalgic are the woody smells of smoke and the sensation of the first misty mornings. At this time the hedgerows are ripe with fruits and berries. The blackberry is a special favourite of china painters, and I have chosen a project which incorporates all aspects of the autumn scene.

PROJECT . . . . *The Season of Mists*

One of my favourite fruits to paint is the blackberry. To make the design more interesting I added a misty scene.

COLOURS USED
soft turquoise · pale green · violet · pink · yellow-green · yellow-brown · maroon/ black-grape · blue · lemon · shading green · yellow-red · black

BRUSHES/ EQUIPMENT
graphite paper · tracing paper · ball point pen · wipe-out tool · ¹/₂in (13mm) flat brush · berry brush (or other small pointed brush) · various other brushes

FIRST FIRE
❋ Trace or sketch the design on to the china.
❋ Using the ¹/₂in (13mm) flat shader brush, apply a slightly textured tint around the design and a little pale yellow in the top left-hand corner to indicate sunlight. Keep

the background colours pale at this stage – suggested colours are soft turquoise, pale green, violet and pink.
❋ Paint the leaves using the same flat shader with yellow-green, and add a touch of yellow-brown. Paint around the bottom of the blackberries with maroon or black-grape then paint their tops with a medium shade of blue.
❋ Use the berry brush to mark out the individual seeds. With light brown, suggest a few stems.
❋ Wipe out the little five-petalled flowers from the wet background colour, and paint their centres with lemon.
❋ While the background is still wet, lightly suggest a misty scene – nothing too definite. Imagine your own scene and paint it in very lightly using a ¹/₂in (13mm) flat brush. It needs to look very relaxed and not overworked with detail.
❋ Fire at 1472°F (800°C).

SECOND FIRE
❋ Apply a deeper colour around the main fruit design, making it darker in the shadow area. Fade the background out towards the edge of the piece but make sure that you keep the area of yellow sunlight.

❖ With shading green, apply a little more colour to the leaves, and paint on some yellow-red and yellow-brown to suggest autumn shades. Apply more black-grape and some black to the berries. Paint shadowy leaves into the wet background and accentuate the flowers and stems. If the scene needs more colour, apply it now.

❖ Fire at 1472°F (800°C).

THIRD FIRE

❖ Deepen the colour of the berries if needed.

❖ Fire at 1436°F (780°C).

Special Items

This selection of projects is concerned with those special items, available to the china painter, which create wonderful surfaces on which to experiment with techniques, colour and design. Their range of use, from the practical beauty of handpainted tiles, through to exciting and dramatic personalized jewellery, means that everyone will find some inspiration within the following pages.

TILES

The use of decorative tiles goes back thousands of years. As early as the fourth millennium BC the Egyptians were using blue glazed bricks to decorate their buildings. In the fourteenth century the technique of making tiles inlaid with different colours was developed. Later, tiles with designs scratched under the glaze were introduced. Potters in Mesopotamia and Assyria, two similar cultures, used coloured glazed bricks in buildings. In China, decorated pottery tablets were laid in tombs, and later coloured tiles were used for roofing. But it was in Mesopotamia and Persia that tile-making reached the zenith of excellence and, from these regions, the skill gradually spread to the Western world.

In the Islamic world, highly decorated ceramic tiles played a major part in the embellishment of buildings and wonderful examples can still be seen in the Middle East. Two of the main pottery-making centres of this area were Baghdad and Basra on the Persian Gulf. Opaque white tin glazes were applied to the pottery tiles after firing, and the tiles were then decorated with coloured glazes and designs, and often given an extra layer of clear glaze.

An important development during the ninth century AD was the use of lustres (see pages 48–51) to decorate tiles. This style of decoration was used almost exclusively by the Islamic potteries for many years. Hundreds of different techniques were used to create original and ornate effects. Tiles were made in all shapes and continuous patterns and some were curved to decorate domes and pillars. Tiles used for flooring and for decorating stoves had to be extremely strong with a hard glaze. They were also made in different thicknesses depending on the surface they were to cover – some tiles were up to 3 inches (7.5 centimetres) thick!

Tiles have also been used for many centuries in the Mediterranean countries, particularly in Italy, Spain and Portugal. In Europe, Holland's Delft pottery has been in the forefront of tile-making. In the United Kingdom, tile-making goes back several centuries to when Flemish potters settled. Later, during the Art and Craft period, the designs of William Morris and William de Morgan influenced the decoration of tiles.

It was during the nineteenth-century Gothic revival that renewed interest was shown in the manufacture of tiles – this later grew into a major industry. Factories such as Doulton, Minton, Maw & Co and many smaller potteries led the field in Europe. Tiles were designed to decorate floors, walls, fireplaces and panels, ranging from just a few tiles with interlinking patterns, to large decorative wall panels consisting of many tiles of all sizes.

DECORATING TILES

Tiles are an excellent shape for beginners to work on – the surface is completely flat and they are easy to hold and to fire in the kiln. Tiles come in many shapes and sizes. I usually start beginners with 6×3in (15×7.5cm) oval or 6in (15cm) round shapes as these provide a more interesting shape than the square tiles. They can then be mounted on wooden bases to make teapot stands, or on velvet ribbon, hanging either singly or in twos or threes on the wall. To create a design for a tray or tabletop, several square tiles can be placed together to form a tile panel which will give a larger decorative effect. Paint personalized wall murals for kitchens or bathrooms.

When painting tile panels, bear in mind that they will have a layer of grouting between and around the tiles which must be taken into account when planning the design. If painting a large panel of, say, twelve tiles, number each one on the back and fire the number on before starting the design. This is to enable you to piece the jigsaw together when the tiles come out of the kiln. Remember that you could be painting the tiles in a different room, usually some way from the kiln, and you will have to transport the tiles from the workplace to the kiln so some special support, for example a tray, may be needed to do this.

If you are painting a large mural, you will need to mix a large quantity of colour beforehand and probably use a sponge or very big brush to apply the colours. You may find the water-based mediums more suitable in this case.

If the design is to include figures, try to place them so that they are not divided by the tiles or the grouting. Although some figures will certainly span two or more tile joints, use your discretion and place them in the best position possible so as not to spoil the effect of the design. If you decided on a 'repeat' design to link the tiles, do not make it too complicated. Something simple can often be more effective.

Avoid using gold, silver or lustres in areas which are to get lots of wear. Having said that, when I was commissioned to paint a mural for Virgin Airlines, mother-of-pearl and platinum were specially requested. After much deliberation I agreed to include them in the design, and after several years of regular cleaning, they still look good. Do not use the non-fire colours on tiles which will be in use, as the design will be removed during cleaning.

TIPS
1 Make sure that the overall pattern links properly.
2 Allow for the grouting between tiles.
3 Try not to split an important part of the design over two tiles.
4 Fire **hot** *(1472°F/800°C) to make sure that the colours go well under the glaze.*

CREATING A REPEAT PATTERN ON A TILE

(Top left) The design roughed out, shows how many 'segments' are needed. (Top right) The tile is divided into eight, in this instance, and the pattern penned in. (Bottom left) With the whole pattern applied and fired, the background is painted in segments, too. (Bottom right) The completed design.

Blue and White Tile Tray

COLOURS USED
mazarine blue ·
medium blue

BRUSHES/ EQUIPMENT
graphite paper ·
tracing paper · ball-
point pen · mapping
pen · dark blue ink ·
No.3 pointed brush

This design was taken from a Famille Verte vase of the period between 1785 and 1800 and is an ideal subject for blue and white tile design. Blue and white never fails to please as it always looks fresh and clean. The handpainted blue and white that came from China was first seen in Europe in the seventeenth century, but only the wealthy minority could afford it. Mass production in Europe became possible with the new transfer printing process. Originally transfer printing was done in black but successful results were obtained by using blue cobalt oxide and the technique quickly spread to the factories such as Worcester and Caughley in Shropshire. Spode perfected the production of bone china in the mid-eighteenth century and this ware, owing to its soft glaze, was the perfect vehicle for transfer printing. Favourite themes were 'Chinoiseries' designs depicting romanticized Western notions of Chinese themes, the most famous being the willow pattern which is a purely Western invention. It is still produced today on everything from soap dishes to tea sets.

Chinese designs gradually faded in popularity, and romantic and rural British scenes took over for a while. Then American themes became popular as the USA started to provide a profitable export trade. For many years I disliked the blue and white style of ware but after studying its history, I began to like and appreciate it and now I actually collect it.

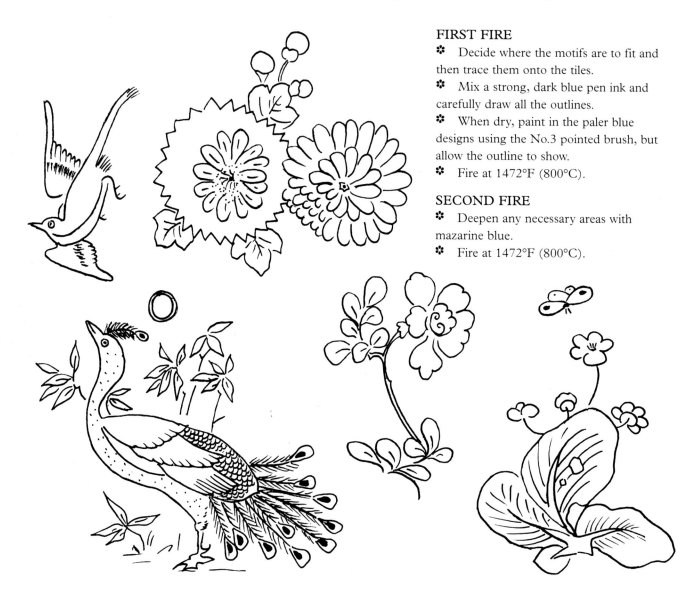

FIRST FIRE

✽ Decide where the motifs are to fit and then trace them onto the tiles.

✽ Mix a strong, dark blue pen ink and carefully draw all the outlines.

✽ When dry, paint in the paler blue designs using the No.3 pointed brush, but allow the outline to show.

✽ Fire at 1472°F (800°C).

SECOND FIRE

✽ Deepen any necessary areas with mazarine blue.

✽ Fire at 1472°F (800°C).

CHINA BOXES

China and porcelain boxes with lids are among my favourite items on which to paint. There are so many lovely shapes to choose from, all of which are easily available from suppliers. Boxes can be obtained in a wide range of sizes, from the tiny 'tooth fairy' shape (approximately thumb-nail size) up to the large 'card boxes', large enough to take two packs of cards – an excellent gift for bridge-playing friends.

There are one or two points to remember when painting boxes. It is important to make sure the design is correctly placed and not lopsided. If the base of the box is to be decorated on the outside, allow the design to flow down in an attractive way. Always paint a small design inside the box, and for an extra surprise for the recipient paint a tiny design inside the lid. When firing the boxes, never fire soft bone china with the lid in place, as the glazes will stick together and you won't be able to remove them without risk of breaking. Porcelain can be safely fired with the lid in position. If in doubt, fire the lids and bases separately.

PROJECT . . . . *Acorn Box*

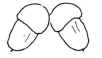

COLOURS USED
yellow-brown ·
chartreuse · moss
green · brown · gold

BRUSHES/ EQUIPMENT
graphite paper ·
tracing paper · ball
point pen · ½in
(13mm) flat brush ·
No.4 pointed brush ·
00 pointed brush ·
various other brushes

FIRST FIRE
❀ Trace the design on to the lid and paint a light wash of colour around the design with the ½in (13mm) flat brush. Keep the colours pale at this stage.
❀ With a No.4 pointed brush apply some chartreuse and yellow-brown to the leaves. Paint the acorn cup with some brown and moss green mixed together.
❀ Paint the acorn with yellow-brown and wipe out a highlight on the side facing the light. Paint in the stems with brown using a 00 pointed brush.

❀ Fire at 1436°F (780°C).

SECOND FIRE
❀ Paint a little more colour onto the leaves using moss green and add some brown to a few leaf edges. Add some yellow-brown to the base of the acorn.
❀ Fire at 1436°F (780°C).

THIRD FIRE
❀ You may add a fine, broken, pen outline with brown if you wish.
❀ Fire at 1436°F (780°C).

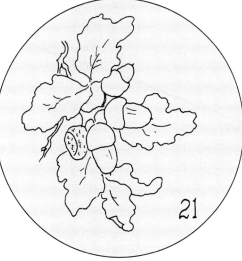

Primrose Box

FIRST FIRE

❖ Sketch or trace the design. Do not include too much detail, this will be done with a brush later (see page 77).

❖ Paint a fine wash of primrose yellow on the flower and pale green on the leaves. Wipe out some highlights on the flowers.

❖ Paint the stems pale green with a 00 pointed brush.

❖ In the centre of the flower, paint a small, round 'button' shape in pale green. Wipe out a tiny highlight.

❖ Fire at 1472°F (800°C).

SECOND FIRE

❖ Using the ½in (13mm) flat brush, paint a pale background around the design, making it darker on the shadow side.

❖ Paint some primrose yellow at the top left of the background to show direction of light.

❖ Add just a little more yellow to the flowers and form a few turnbacks by painting under the turned-back petal with yellow-brown.

❖ Shade the leaves with moss green with a No.4 pointed brush, using a dabbing motion to achieve the curled effect.

❖ Using the wipe-out tool, take out the centre vein, exposing the pale green underneath which has already been fired. With yellow-brown, paint the centre.

❖ Fire at 1436°F (780°C).

THIRD FIRE

❖ Using a fine pen and some pen oil mixed with moss green, draw a fine, broken line around the design. Deepen any shadow area in the background.

❖ Paint a small design inside the box.

❖ Fire at 1436°F (780°C).

COLOURS USED

primrose yellow · pale green · moss green · yellow-brown · turquoise

BRUSHES/ EQUIPMENT

graphite paper · tracing paper · ball point pen · mapping pen · pen oil · 00 pointed brush · ½in (13mm) flat brush · No.4 pointed brush · various other brushes

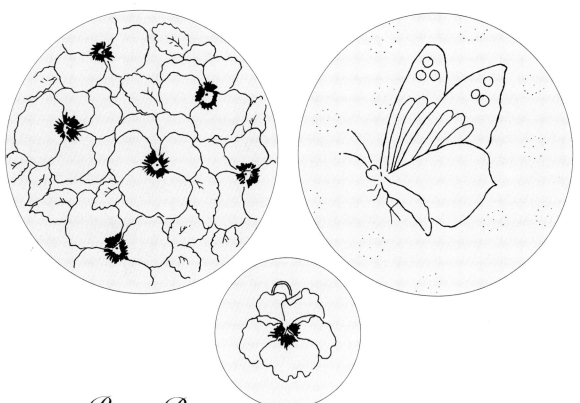

PROJECT . . . .

COLOURS USED
yellow-red · American Beauty · black-grape · black · yellow · malachite · leaf green · mauve · liquid bright gold · burnishing gold

BRUSHES/ EQUIPMENT
graphite paper · tracing paper · ball-point pen · wipe-out tool · fine mapping pen · ¹/₂in (13mm) flat brush · 00 pointed brush · various other brushes

Pansy Box

Before you commence the flower, study a real pansy and note how the 'whiskers' on the faces are a vibrant, crisp dark colour with a yellow centre.

FIRST FIRE
❋ Carefully trace the pansies on to the lid and allow one or two petals and leaves to overlap on to the base of the box.
❋ Using the ¹/₂in (13mm) flat brush, paint the back two petals of each flower first in American Beauty. Do not paint the 'whiskers' yet.
❋ Paint the other three petals with yellow, and add a touch of yellow-brown to some edges.
❋ Paint the centres in yellow and wipe out the little inverted 'v' shape in the centre with a wipe-out tool.
❋ Paint some pansies mauve and black-grape.
❋ Paint the leaves with leaf green.
❋ Fire at 1472°F (800°C).

SECOND FIRE
❋ Add more colour to the pansies and, using a very fine 00 pointed brush and deepest black paint, form the 'whiskers'.

These must be crisp and clean, and not be allowed to run into any wet colour on the petals or you will get a messy looking centre.
❋ Using a No.1 pointed brush, paint the spaces between the pansies with malachite.
❋ Paint the design inside the box.
❋ Fire at 1436°F (780°C).

THIRD FIRE
❋ Using burnishing gold and a fine mapping pen, outline each flower very carefully.
❋ With liquid bright gold, paint the base of the box.
❋ Fire at 1400°F (760°C).

FOURTH FIRE
❋ Apply the burnishing gold to the base of the box.
❋ Fire at 1400°F (760°C).
❋ Burnish after firing with a burnishing brush or burnishing sand.

Butterfly Box

This design is first penned on before adding colour. If you use a fast-drying pen oil you can paint the colours and do the penwork on the first fire. If you use a pen oil which does not dry until fired, you will need to complete the penned outline and fire it, then paint the colour on the next firing. The mother-of-pearl lustre was applied on a completely separate firing.

Butterflies can be painted any colour you wish, except of course when painting specific species. The body is almost always very dark, either black or dark brown. Butterflies have little 'blobs' on their antennae, moths do not. If any part of the butterfly is black, then make it a deep opaque black, not a wishy-washy grey colour. Your butterflies should be vibrant, with a zing.

COLOURS USED
yellow-brown · yellow-red · soft turquoise · black · mother-of-pearl lustre · halo fluid

BRUSHES/ EQUIPMENT
graphite paper · tracing paper · ball point pen · mapping pen · pen oil

FIRST FIRE
❉ Carefully trace the design on to the lid of the box.

❉ Mix pen oil with black paint to make a fluid, workable consistency. Outline the butterfly with a fine, clean line.

❉ When it is completely dry, fill in the colours on the butterfly. I used yellow-brown, yellow-red, and turquoise. If you are using black for a wing pattern, make it deep black and do not allow it to run into any other colours.

❉ Fire at 1472°F (800°C).

SECOND FIRE
❉ Deepen any colours on the butterfly.

❉ Paint a design inside the box.

❉ Fire at 1436°F (780°C).

THIRD FIRE
❉ Apply a coat of mother-of-pearl lustre around the butterfly and box base.

❉ When almost dry, using a fine brush, apply the halo lustre fluid in tiny drops; it will spread to make small perfect circles in the lustre (practise on a spare tile first).

❉ When completely dry, pen the little dots just inside the halo circles.

❉ Fire at 1400°F (760°C).

TIPS
1 Always paint a design inside the box.
2 If the design is to trail from the lid on to the base of the box, make sure that the design matches where it meets.
3 Do not fire bone china boxes with the lids on.
4 A small piece needs as much forethought as a large one.
5 Keep any spare lids or bases – they are useful if you have a breakage.
6 When buying boxes, make sure that the lid fits the base as well as possible and that the box is not misshapen. Round bone china boxes are rarely perfect.

1

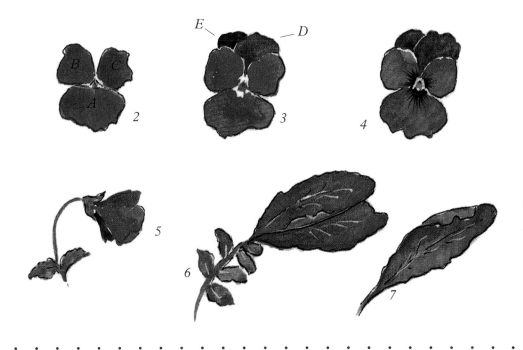

PAINTING PANSIES
1 Upturned 'v' with dot in centre forms nucleus of the flower.
2 Start with large base petal A and add petals B and C.
3 Fill in two back petals D and E.
4 This shows the pansy with turned-back petals and central 'whiskers'.
5 A bud with two base leaves.
6 Leaves in groups.
7 Single leaf.

PAINTING ACORNS

1 The acorn in its cup.
2 The empty cup – the outside is rough and slightly curly, while the inside is smooth.
3 Acorns on the stem – they usually grow in little groups.
4 and 5 Oak leaves. Note the curvy edges – a lovely shape to draw and paint.

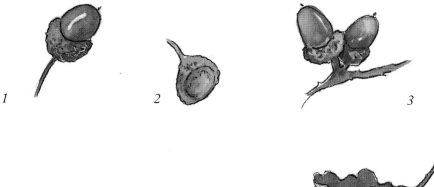

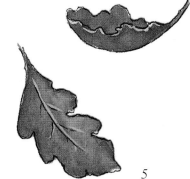

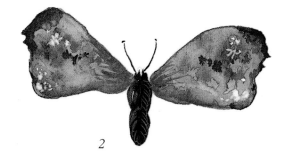

PAINTING A BUTTERFLY

1 Paint in the body using simple comma strokes.
2 Add the top wings using a larger brush, copying the pattern from one side to the other.
3 The lower wings are painted in a similar way.
4 Side view of a butterfly.

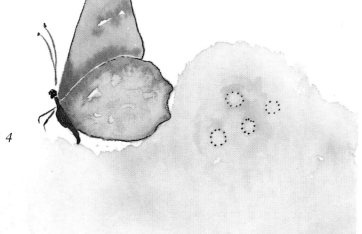

FIGURINES

Figurines can be quite tedious to paint, but they offer a challenge and are extremely rewarding when they turn out well. When choosing a figure to paint, make sure that the face is clearly defined and that there are no unglazed areas on the piece. Often, noses are not properly defined and after painting the figure will have a 'pug nose' appearance. Make sure that the figure does not tilt to one side but stands up straight.

Apply the colour with a soft, flat brush then blend the wet paint with a blending brush. If there are large areas of plain colour to fill, it is often better to apply the paint with a large, soft brush and then pad with a synthetic sponge. If there are any parts you wish to paint around, cover them with masking fluid.

Faces should be slightly understated – do not make the features too prominent and do not apply too much detail. Avoid applying heavy colours to this area – keep them delicate, smooth and subtle.

If the figure is difficult to hold whilst painting, you can secure it to the unglazed side of an ordinary tile with Blu-Tack – the figure then becomes easier to turn. You can fire it with the Blu-Tack in place as this will burn to ash in the kiln and do the piece no harm. The way you work will dictate the number of firings needed; you may find it easier to give the piece several fires and complete one portion at a time, but do as much as you can without smudging the wet paint. Leave any gold or lustrework until the last fire. As most figurines are made of bone china, do not let them touch in the kiln or they will stick together.

TIPS
1   If a section of the figure is slightly flawed, keep the colours pale.
2   Do not attempt to paint the whole piece at once – complete one side at a time.
3   Check for any faults before you start painting.
4   If there are any rough spots on the china surface, do not apply any colour at all to this part – leave it white. It will look worse if you try to disguise it.
5   If you fire a figure secured to Blu-Tack, be sure to brush out the ash from the kiln after firing.

JEWELLERY

❋

There is nothing more rewarding than to receive compliments on your jewellery if you have made it yourself. There are countless shapes and styles of porcelain jewellery available to decorate – you can really enjoy yourself by experimenting with your own designs.

Porcelain medallions come in a variety of sizes, from ½in (1cm) to 5in (12.5cm). Adapt the larger pieces into items such as buckles, hair slides and brooches. Jewellery findings (the metal shapes into which the porcelain is glued) are also available and in dozens of shapes – in base metal, such as chrome and gilt, in sterling silver, and also in nine carat gold. The chains for necklaces can be purchased in standard sizes, 16–18in (40–46cm), or by the inch. The painting should be completed *before* gluing the porcelain into the findings as the metal would melt in the kiln. Porcelain bracelets and earrings are also available for painting, and matching sets make beautiful and unique gifts.

I have sketched some ideas for you, but I am sure that you will have no trouble discovering exciting ideas of your own. Some of the designs shown have been made using I-Relief and flaking compounds; for details of how to use these techniques see 'Special Effects' (pages 64–5). You can also try using lustres, gold and silver.

A RANGE OF JEWELLERY IDEAS:
1 An abstract face brooch. Textured gold, orange lustre and blue lustres have been used.
2 A variation on 1 but showing features, decorated with fired-on glass.
3 Earrings made using fine-textured sand and fired-on glass.
4 A round brooch with various lustres and gold, and with fired-on glass.
5 A mother-of-pearl brooch with fine textured gold and just a little black onglaze enamel.

1

2

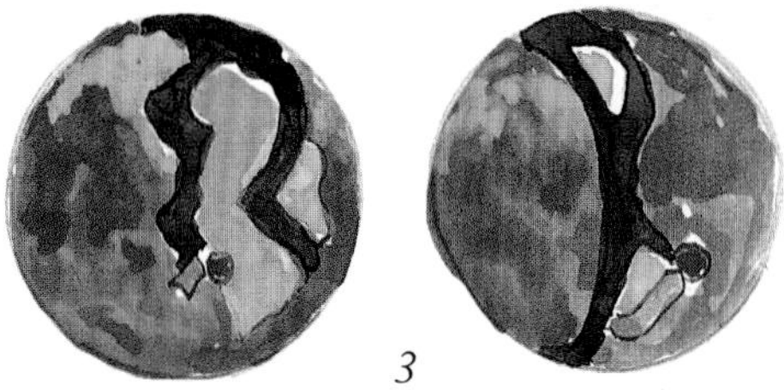

3

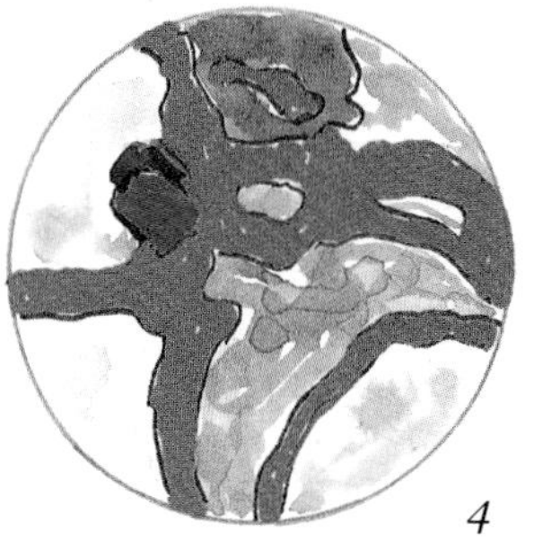

4

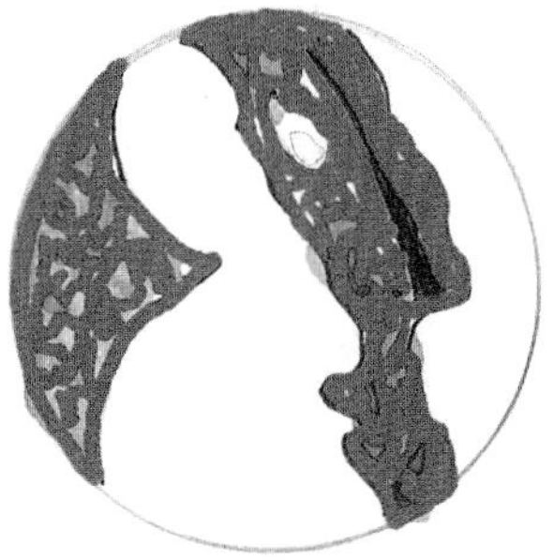

5

1 Do not use heavy medallions for necklaces as they will fall forwards when you lean over and the porcelain will break.
2 To make painting easier, fix the porcelain medallions to the unfired side of a tile with glue or Blu-Tack and fire them. The adhesive will burn to a white powder in the kiln and will not harm the porcelain.
3 If your brooch medallion has a diameter wider than 2in (5cm), attach the pin fastener towards the top of the piece to hold it firmly upright.
4 Before gluing, roughen the surface of the porcelain and the metal finding with sandpaper for better adhesion.

Most of these designs could be done using the non-fire colours. However, as jewellery undergoes a lot of wear and tear, it would be better if the pieces were painted in the traditional way and fired in a kiln.

1 This cat was painted with opaque colour and fired first at 1436°F (780°C). The bright oranges and red used for the background needed a cooler firing at 1400°F (760°C).

2 The figure was painted opaque black with a solid colour, then fired at 1436°F (780°C). The white penwork was done on a separate fire, and the blue marbled lustre added.

3 Pen the entire design in black and when this is dry, fill in the colours. Fire at 1436°F (780°C).

4 Paint this design and fire once.

5 Pen the design and when dry, paint the leaves with chartreuse, hibiscus and pansy purple. Then with a fine brush paint the black background and fire at 1472°F (800°C).

6 Paint the porcelain with yellow and brown, and drop in a little turpentine. After firing add white enamel and the little stones and fire again.

7 Paint these violets with mauve, and then paint the leaves. The background was done with pansy purple and yellow and the piece was fired at 1436°F (780°C).

8 Mask out the circle and paint the rest of the medallion with black. Remove the masking and paint the black rose. After firing add the white enamel rose.

9 Paint each bracelet medallion with a different flower.

1

2

3

4

5

6

7

8

9

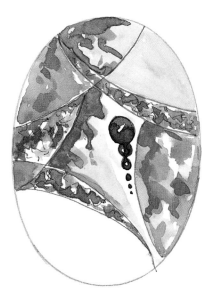

*1 An oval medallion
with textured gold,
lustres and glass beads.
2 This size of oval is
suitable for a portrait.
3 Simple flower designs
can be quite effective.
4 A long, oval
medallion suitable for a
pendant.
5 One large flower on a
groundlaid background.
6 Earrings with blue
lustre, onglaze colours
and a little textured
gold.
7 Earring with blue
and purple lustres.
Gold was added on the
second fire with a fine
brush.
8 A teardrop-shaped
pendant with penwork
orchids.*

1

2

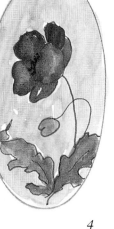

3

4

5

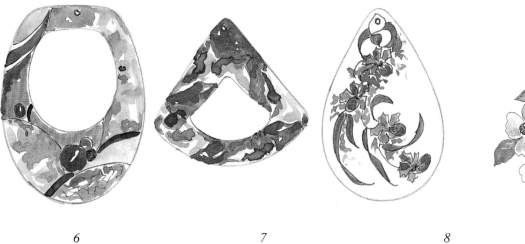

6

7

8

TESTED TIPS

1   Never work in a dusty atmosphere.
2   Always clean and condition your brushes after use.
3   Keep your working surfaces uncluttered.
4   Mix paints to the consistency of toothpaste.
5   Always keep a separate brush for gold and lustres.
6   Buy the best brushes you can afford.
7   You can pick up an unwanted hair which has fallen onto the wet paint with the point of a wax pencil.
8   Always paint on clean, undamaged china.
9   If using soft English bone china, do not let the pieces touch in the kiln or they will stick together.
10 If pinks look yellowish after firing you have probably not used a high enough temperature.
11 If your colours chip after firing, they were applied too thickly or fired too hot.
12 If your pencil design shows after firing you are not firing hot enough.
13 You may place the painted pieces in your own oven at 302°F (150°C) to dry the paint – do not be alarmed if it turns a strange colour, as it will right itself during firing at the correct temperature.
14 Fat oil can be made by evaporating turpentine.
15 The gold colours (pinks, rubies, violets) need more mixing than the other colours.
16 Make a colour chart of all your colours.
17 A little yellow in the background brings sunlight into a design.
18 Keep the darkest background under the main part of the design.
19 Decide from which side the light is falling and keep shadows in the appropriate places.
20 Backgrounds may be padded with silk for a matt finish.
21 Always work with as large a brush as you can handle.
22 Use grey when shading white flowers.
23 Keep your designs uncomplicated and clean.
24 Follow the contour of the china with the design.
25 Do not eat, drink or smoke while handling paints.
26 A dash of violet is a useful colour where white flowers are to be used.
27 Use some of the colours in your main design in the background.
28 A little flux added to your mixed paint will give a 'glossy' effect after firing.
29 Keep finger marks off the areas to be painted with gold or lustres.
30 Fired gold smears can be removed with a gold eraser.
31 Use a mapping pen for gold scrolls.
32 Try a scene in monochrome (different shades of one colour).
33 Golds and lustres sit on top of the glaze; coloured enamels are absorbed into it.
34 Do not let your gold come into contact with any unfired colour.
35 Place your bottle of gold in a wedge of plasticine to avoid spillages.
36 A little gold mixed with silver will prevent tarnishing.
37 Silver looks beautiful with green.
38 To thin gold and silver use a precious metal thinner.
39 Always wear a face mask when using paint in its powdered form to avoid inhalation.
40 Turpentine can be re-used if sediment is allowed to settle on the bottom.
41 If your lustres are streaky, a coat of mother-of-pearl over the top works wonders.
42 Too much oil in the raised enamel will cause it to blister.
43 Do not blame your teacher for imperfections which appear during firing. They were there before, but could not be seen.
44 If your teacher refuses to show or explain techniques such as gilding and firing, change your teacher.
45 Most of all, enjoy your painting!

QUESTION TIME

How can I be sure when my paints are correctly ground and mixed?
When all grainy particles have been eliminated and paint is at a toothpaste consistency, ie when it will not shake off the palette knife.

Can I paint one coat of gold over another that has not been fired?
Yes. When the first layer has completely dried, apply an even second coat, not too thickly, and fire as normal.

Does my paint have to be dry before I fire it?
No, you can fire it immediately.

I painted a plate twelve months ago. Is it too late to fire it?
No, provided you have kept off the dust you can fire as usual.

If there is a power failure during firing, will my pieces be ruined?
No, this will not affect your pieces at all; just re-fire in the normal way.

What design is good for a beginner to use on a tea set?
A beginner should never attempt a tea or dinner set; only disappointment can result. Wait until you are more competent before tackling such a complex job.

What is the difference between grounding and dusting?
Groundlaying is a method of achieving a rich, dark background in one fire by applying dry, sieved powdered paint over a layer of special grounding oil. Dusting is the application of powdered paint over the selected painted area after drying and before firing; this gives dark accents where you want them in one fire, which is very tricky to do. A drying medium such as copaiba is necessary for this.

My gold is too thick; what can I do?
Dilute with a tiny drop of precious metal thinner, never turpentine.

Can I touch up the worn gold on an old piece?
Yes. Just apply the gold as usual and fire. But be aware that damage can result if the piece is very old.

Can I re-touch with paint where the colour has chipped off?
You may be lucky, but usually once the colour has chipped off it takes the glaze with it so there is nothing for the paint to adhere to. You can try adding some flux to your ground colour, as this sometimes helps. Try one of the non-fire colours.

After firing, some of the colour rubbed off, and my pencil marks were still visible. What did I do wrong?
Your china was not fired hot enough. Use more heat.

After firing, my colours all looked dull and not glossy.
The answer is the same as above – underfired; re-fire at a higher temperature.

My colours look too pale after firing. What causes this?
Too little paint used in mixing or too much oil used in painting; you can only have your colours as strong as the paint you put on. But it is better to have it this way than for it to be too heavy, as you can always add more colour on subsequent firings.

My piece painted with non-fire colours has come out with smears and streaks – what did I do wrong?
You probably used too much paint and then had trouble smoothing it out – try painting over it again with a little of the same colour.

When I removed my pieces painted with non-fire colours from my oven I could easily rub the design off. What went wrong?
You did not have the oven hot enough. Follow manufacturers' instructions.

Why can't I use the pieces painted with non-fire colours to eat and drink from?
Because these colours are acrylic and not mineral onglaze enamels. The acrylic colours cannot fuse with the glaze in the same way as the onglaze enamels, which actually sink under the glaze when fired in a kiln at around 1436°F (780°C). The acrylic colours bake in a domestic oven at the lower temperature of approximately 348°F (175°C).

GLOSSARY

ANISEED Oil used as a penwork medium.

BAT The shelf of a kiln.

BISQUE China, porcelain or pottery which is unglazed. Pottery is often decorated in this state, but china and porcelain are decorated after the glaze has been added and fired.

BONE CHINA Translucent white ware. Made from 50% animal bone, 25% china stone, 25% china clay. Decorative firing is done at 1400–1472°F (760–800°C). Bone is expensive to use, and substitutes are sometimes used instead, but true whiteness is never achieved without it.

BUNG (VENT) The plug of ceramic material which is inserted into the hole in the kiln to seal it after all noxious gases have escaped.

CERAMICS A term covering all types of pottery and porcelain.

CHINA General term used to describe the wares on which we paint because China was the first country to make such material. See also BONE CHINA.

CHINAGRAPH PENCIL Special soft pencil used on porcelain.

CLOSED MEDIUM An oil which dries quickly, before firing, such as fat oil.

CLOVE OIL Used to keep colours open.

CONES Small ceramic shapes, usually triangular, designed to melt in the kiln at a pre-set temperature.

COPAIBA Thick oil used as a painting medium.

DECAL Another name for a transfer. See TRANSFER

EARTHENWARE An opaque ware. Has a fairly 'open' body which easily absorbs water. It consists of 25% Ball clay, 25% China clay, 35% flint and 15% China stone.

EGGSHELL Hard paste porcelain of exceptional thinness.

ENAMELS Pigments made from metallic and mineral oxides and used to decorate porcelain and china, often called onglaze enamels when used by china painters because they are painted over the glaze.

GLAZE Glassy substance applied to biscuit ware giving a water-repellent covering. It is made from purified sand and water.

GOLD Precious metal used to decorate ceramics. Either 12–15% gold, or 22 carat.

GOLD ERASER A rubber which removes unwanted fired-on gold smears. It also removes fired lustres and platinum.

GRAPHITE PAPER A carbon-like paper with a graphite covering, especially suitable for transferring patterns in china painting.

HARD PASTE PORCELAIN Colours lie more on top of the glaze than with bone china. It is made from 50% china clay, 30% china stone, 20% flint. Decorative firing at 1472–1594°F (800–850°C).

HIGHLIGHTS Light areas wiped out of wet paint to achieve a light effect.

KILN Oven necessary to fire ceramics to make a painted design permanent.

KILN SITTER A device fitted to kilns which will collapse a small cone at the required temperature, switching off the current so that over-firing cannot occur.

LAVENDER OIL Oil used to mix with other oils to achieve a good painting consistency.

LUSTRE Made from metallic oxides

suspended in liquid which fire away in the kiln, leaving a coat of iridescent metal.

MASKING FLUID Liquid used to mask out areas not to be painted.

MEDIUM The name given to any oil used to facilitate china painting.

MIXING MEDIUM The oil used to grind the onglaze colours.

NATURALISTIC PAINTING A term used by china painters to describe the style of painting where a subtle background is added.

NON-FIRE COLOURS Acrylic colours in liquid form which are baked in a domestic oven after application. These colours are only semi-permanent.

ONGLAZE ENAMELS Powdered colours which are painted over the glaze of china and porcelain. They are also available in a water-based form and should be fired between 1382–1562°F (750–850°C).

OPEN MEDIUM An oil which takes a long time to dry, or doesn't dry until fired.

PADDING A method of smoothing the painted colour with a silk pad or sponge.

PAINTING MEDIUM The oil used to lubricate your brush before dipping it into the mixed colour.

PEN OIL An oil which is mixed with onglaze colours to a consistency suitable to flow through a fine nib.

PLATINUM Precious metal which gives a soft silver shade after firing.

PORCELAIN A strong off-white, hard-bodied ware. See also HARD PASTE PORCELAIN and SOFT PASTE PORCELAIN.

POTTERY Soft glazed ware, usually decorated under the glaze.

PYROMETER A temperature indicator and controller for the kiln.

RAISED ENAMEL A white enamel powder with which to make raised designs.

RAISED PASTE A yellow powder with which to make raised designs as a base for gold.

SILK PAD A piece of pure silk wrapped over a wad of cotton wool. Used for padding and smoothing colour.

SOFT PASTE PORCELAIN Similar to hard paste porcelain, but the body is more granular, and colours sink into the glaze more.

TINTED BACKGROUND A smooth light-coloured background applied and fired before adding a design.

TRANSFER Also called a decal. A pre-printed design for use in china painting.

TURPENTINE Pure turpentine is used to clean brushes.

WIPE-OUT A method of taking off wet colour with a cleaned brush, exposing the white china below.

LIST OF SUPPLIERS

ORGANIZATIONS AND MAGAZINES

Contact with other china painters is essential to the development of your art, and for this reason I am including a short list of porcelain organizations. If you contact any of these, they will put you in touch with other painters in your area. A stamped addressed envelope is appreciated when possible.

British China and Porcelain Artists Association
Non-profit making official UK organization : Regional shows and seminars : Annual convention : Clubs : Diploma examination : Magazine *British China Painter* (quarterly)
Contact: Sheila Southwell, 7 West Street, Burgess Hill, West Sussex, RH15 8NN. Tel: 01444 244307

Westfield House China Painting School
Residential courses : Magazine *British Porcelain Artist*
Westfield House, North Avenue, Wakefield, Yorkshire

China Decorator Magazine
3200 North Shingle Road, Shingle Springs, California, CA 95682, USA

IPAT International Porcelain Artists and Teachers
Magazine *Porcelain Artist*
7424 Greenville Avenue, Dallas 75231, Texas, USA

Australian Porcelain Decorator **Magazine**
P O Box 156, Walkerville, South Australia

Porselans Maling **Magazine**
2260 Kirkenger, Norway

Scandinavian Porcelain Magazine **(SPM)**
Martinkyläntie 41, Finland 01720, Vantaa, Finland

Het Porselein Schilder Genootschap **(PSG)**
Betsy Kes, Woudweg 73, 7381 BA Klarenbeek, Netherlands.

SUPPLIERS OF CHINA PAINTING MATERIALS
UNITED KINGDOM

Art Graphique, Unit 2, Poulton Close, Dover, Kent. *(Non-fire colours)*

The Art Shop, 31 Albert Road, Colne, Lancashire. Tel: 01282 862467. *(Books: Bone china)*

The Craft Centre, Ganton, Scarborough, Yorkshire, YO12 4NR. Tel: 01944 710132. *(General supplies)*

Mid Cornwall Gallery, Biscovey, Par, Cornwall, PL24 2EG. Tel: 0172681 2131. *(General supplies)*

Marisa D'Aprano Studios, 34 Coombe Lane, West Wimbledon, London, SW20 0LA. Tel: 081-879 0277. *(China and glass colours)*

H.R. Edge, 158 Star & Garter Road, Longton, Stoke-on-Trent, ST3 7HN. *(General supplies)*

Green and Stone Artists Supplies, London and Chichester. *(Non-fire ceramic colours)*

HELD of Harrogate, 16 Station Parade, Harrogate, North Yorkshire, HG1 1UE. Tel: 01423 504772. *(General supplies)*

Howe & Ware, 42 Gladys Avenue, North End, Portsmouth, PO2 9BG. Tel: 01705 661987. *(General supplies)*

Lalco Ltd, 4 Elsing Street, Fenton, Stoke-on-Trent, ST4 2PR. Tel: 0782 44858. *(Transfers: Supplies)*

Pilling Pottery, School Lane, Pilling, Garstang, Lancashire, PR3 6HB. Tel: 01253 790307. *(Kilns)*

Potclays, Brick Kiln Lane, Etruria, Stoke-on-Trent, Staffs. Tel: 01782 219816. *(Kilns)*

Potterycrafts, Campbells Road,
Stoke-on-Trent, Staffs, ST4 4ET :
105 Minet Road, London, SW9 7WH.
(General supplies)

Recollect, The Old Village School,
London Road, Sayers Common,
West Sussex. Tel: 01273 833314.
(Doll-making courses/supplies)

Sheila Southwell (IPAT & BCPAA
Dip), 7 West Street, Burgess Hill,
West Sussex. Tel: 01444 244307.
(Books : Tuition : Annual show)

Sylvia & Nichola (Sallyport Supplies),
163 Tankerville Drive, Leigh on Sea,
Essex, SS9 3DB.
Tel: 01702 73928.
(Porcelain and general supplies)

Dorothy Wallace, Rose View,
Blitterlees, Siloth, Cumbria.
Tel: 01697 331804
(Studies and ghostline transfers)

Westview Studios, 59 Broadway West,
Leigh on Sea, Essex, SS9 2BX.
Tel: 01702 712788.
*(General supplies : E.S. colours :
Non-fire colours)*

USA

Jean Beebe, P O Box 17, Brookings,
Oregon 97415.
(Special texture materials : Supplies)

Joyce Berlew, Country Art Studio,
Box 788, Moravia, NY 13118.
(Colours : Brushes : Mediums, etc)

Cridge Inc, Dept. B594, Box 210,
Morrisville, PA 19067.
(Porcelain jewellery)

House of Clay, 1100 N.W.30th,
Oklahoma City, Oklahoma.
(Porcelain and supplies)

Renaldys, 277 Park Street, Troy,
Michigan.
(General supplies)

Rynnes China Co, 222 West 8 Mile
Road, Hazel Park, Michigan 48030
(Porcelain and supplies)

CANADA

The Borland Group, 309 Forest Drive,
Kitchener, Ontario.
(Jewellery supplies)

AUSTRALIA

Bettes Porcelain Shop,
558 Glenferrie Road, Hawthorn,
Victoria 3122.

Gilberton Gallery,
2 Walkerville Terrace, South Australia.

Russell Cowan, 12 Leeds Street,
Rhodes, NSW 2138.
(General supplies)

SCANDINAVIA

AB JA Akesson, Box 36 S, 2442l,
Kavlinge, Sweden.

Bogapott Pikkjalg 9, Tallinna, Estonia.

Global Hobby Engros o/s Mohlenpris
Hovegaard, P O B 2687, N 5026,
Bergen, Norway.

Keskuskatv 7, 00100 Helsinki, Finland.

Max Kopp, verpet Industriomrade,
N1540 Vestby, Norway.
(Porcelain)

E. S. Schjernings Farver, Osteralle,
P O 119, Denmark, Ebeltoft.
*(Manufacturers of E.S. Colours and
Lustres (non-toxic)*

GERMANY

C Kreul, Postf 229, 8550 Forcheim.
(E.S. Colours and supplies)

NETHERLANDS

E. S. Colours Benelux b.v.,
Mrs N. v.d. Pas, Oranjestraat 50,
3991 BA Barendrecht, Netherlands.

INDEX